GCSE SKILLS

SPOKEN LANGUAGE STUDY

Ellie Aslin
Dan Clayton
Julia Glozier
Series Editor: Imelda Pilgrim

Nelson Thornes

Teacher's Book

Text © Ellie Aslin, Dan Clayton and Julia Glozier 2013
Original illustrations © Nelson Thornes Ltd 2013

The right of Ellie Aslin, Dan Clayton and Julia Glozier to be identified as authors of this work has been asserted by them in accordance with the Copyright, Designs and Patents Act 1988.

All rights reserved. No part of this publication may be reproduced or transmitted in any form or by any means, electronic or mechanical, including photocopy, recording or any information storage and retrieval system, without permission in writing from the publisher or under licence from the Copyright Licensing Agency Limited, of Saffron House, 6–10 Kirby Street, London, EC1N 8TS.

Any person who commits any unauthorised act in relation to this publication may be liable to criminal prosecution and civil claims for damages.

Published in 2013 by:
Nelson Thornes Ltd
Delta Place
27 Bath Road
CHELTENHAM
GL53 7TH
United Kingdom

13 14 15 16 17 / 10 9 8 7 6 5 4 3 2 1

A catalogue record for this book is available from the British Library

ISBN 978 1 4085 1915 8

Page make-up and illustrations by Fakenham Prepress Solutions

Printed in China

Contents

Introduction		iv

Section A: Spoken language skills — 1

Unit 1	Non-fluency features: Making it up as you go along	1
Unit 2	Interaction and the structure of talk: Following the rules	7
Unit 3	Lexis: The words we use	12
Unit 4	Grammar and structure: Stories, text and tweets	17
Unit 5	Planned and unplanned speech: The right words at the right time	22
Unit 6	Implied meanings: Why don't you say what you mean?	28
Unit 7	Attitudes to spoken language: 'It ain't what you say, it's the way that you say it'	34

Section B: Schemes of work — 37

The language of education: teachers and students	37
The language of home and family	40
The language of interviews	42
Studying the language of reality television	45
Analysing scripted language	47
The language of different social groups	49
Attitudes to spoken language use	51
Multimodal language: tweets, texts and technology	53

Appendices – Spoken language transcripts — 55

Unit 1	Non-fluency features: Making it up as you go along	55
Unit 2	Interaction and the structure of talk: Following the rules	63
Unit 3	Lexis: The words we use	72
Unit 4	Grammar and structure: Stories, texts and tweets	78
Unit 5	Planned and unplanned speech: The right words at the right time	84
Unit 6	Implied meanings: Why don't you say what you mean?	93
Unit 7	Attitudes to spoken language: 'It ain't what you say, it's the way that you say it'	99

Glossary	103

Introduction

The study of spoken language has been a requirement of the GCSE English Language specifications since 2010 and is covered by Assessment Objective 2:

- Understand variations in spoken language, explaining why language changes in relation to contexts.
- Evaluate the impact of spoken language choices in their own and others' use.

These resources have been written to introduce your students to, and support them in, the study of spoken language. The transcripts and activities have been put together to develop your students' knowledge and build their skills so that they can analyse speech effectively. More specifically, the resources aim to:

- help students understand the way that spoken language differs from other forms of language
- develop their awareness of some of the typical features of spoken language
- encourage students to explore the different factors that influence how people speak, interact and respond to one another
- give students advice about how to approach analysing examples of spoken language.

The Student Book

The Student Book is divided into seven units, each of which focuses on a different aspect of spoken language. Each unit begins with an annotated example demonstrating how to analyse the details of spoken language, and the glossary of keywords provides the vocabulary needed to talk about spoken language precisely.

The examples of spoken language that have been included come from a variety of situations. There are conversations between family and friends, interactions in schools and interviews, speech transcribed from radio and TV, as well as scripted forms like play scripts and speeches.

The carefully structured activities that accompany these examples will help students to build their understanding gradually and give them opportunities to develop key skills in speaking and listening, reading and writing. All students should be able to attempt the first/introductory activities in each section; the activities then progress through to more challenging and sophisticated analysis

later in each unit to stretch more able students and to build links towards students of spoken language at GCSE and beyond.

All Student Book units include:

Activity

Activities to develop and reinforce the skills focus of the unit.

Stretch yourself

Extension activities to take the analysis of a transcript further.

Check your learning

A list of points at the end of the unit that summarise what students have covered.

Key terms

Terms students will find useful to be able to define and understand.

The Teacher Book

The Teacher Book supports the Student Book in several important ways.

- It provides commentaries on all the transcripts and activities, which are detailed enough to support less experienced or non-specialist teachers.
- It suggests Schemes of Work built around common themes in the study of spoken language, to help you draw together the resources from the Student Book into a teaching sequence.
- All the transcripts from the Student Book are included in full on the worksheets. These can be used by students for annotation and analysis.

The transcripts and activities in these resources have been selected to appeal to GCSE students and to provide clear progression and skills development, although no one textbook can account for the wide range of young people encountered in the classroom. You know your students best, so be prepared to be selective, to introduce your own transcripts and activities as appropriate and to encourage your students to source their own materials for research and analysis.

1 Non-fluency features: Making it up as you go along

AO focus

AO2:

- Understand variations in spoken language, explaining why language changes in relation to contexts.
- Evaluate the impact of spoken language choices in their own and others' use.

In this unit your students will:

- become more familiar with the features that disrupt the flow of spontaneous speech, and which can contribute to spoken language appearing to be less standard than written forms
- learn to identify a range of non-fluency and structural features
- focus on pauses and fillers, repairs and corrections, overlapping and sequencing
- learn to examine these features in context, looking for patterns in language and reasons for the presence of non-fluency features.

Key terms

Key terms the students are introduced to in this unit:

- Transcript
- Utterance
- Overlapping
- Voiced pause
- Filler
- Context
- Spontaneous speech
- False start
- Repair
- Tone

Transcripts included in this unit

An interview: James being interviewed about his hobbies and pastimes

At a beauty pageant: Miss South Carolina responds to a question

The Only Way is Essex: two girls chatting

Reality talent show: contestants explain their experiences and friendship

A job interview: an applicant thinks on his feet

Mother and daughter interaction: fitting a hearing aid

Friends disagree: criticising and backtracking

The Jonas Brothers: recounting an unusual event

A committee meeting: conflict in discussion

A family breakfast scenario: multiple conversations

See pp55–62 for photocopiable versions of these transcripts for students to work on.

Getting started

The worked example at the beginning of the unit features a transcription of an informal interview. The questions asked by the interviewer are likely to have been semi-planned and they are generally open-ended to encourage longer responses. The topic (internet use) is not too specialist or challenging. Throughout the interaction there are several ways in which the fluency of each speaker's language is disrupted. The annotations describe these small disruptions in detail, suggesting possible reasons for their occurrence.

Review and reflect

An introductory task: encouraging students to become more aware of the fluency (or lack of!) in their own speech.

In the style of a well-known radio programme, *Just a Minute*, students should attempt to speak for as long as they can on a specific topic, without hesitation, repetition or deviation. This could be organised as a small group activity. Each person in the group should be timed to see how long they can talk on the given topic ('the best invention ever', 'school uniform', 'summer holidays', 'my favourite dinner', etc.) As soon as they slip up by pausing, repeating key words or going off topic, their turn is over. Whoever speaks the longest wins the round. Incorrect challenges to the current speaker mean the challenger loses a point and the speaker can start from scratch. It could culminate with the best speakers from each group going into a final round together. Using hand-held stopwatches or a large stop-clock displayed on the whiteboard will make it easier to monitor the times and may add to the sense of competition.

This has the potential to be competitive and noisy, but should illustrate the point that achieving fluency of spoken language is pretty difficult!

GCSE Spoken Language Skills
Section A: Spoken language skills

Mind the gap

Miss South Carolina

This transcript features a beauty pageant contestant responding to a question about American geographical awareness. It demonstrates the use of voiced pauses and filler phrases.

Activity 1

a There are:

   i seven micropauses

   ii six voiced pauses.

b Stock phrases like: 'I personally believe', 'out there' and 'like such as' are being used to fill out the response. It could be argued, of course, that the whole response is padding (the only vaguely logical part of the response seems to be that some people don't have maps!).

c Accept any descriptions that acknowledge this is a confusing, poorly structured response. To her credit, Miss South Carolina responds at length and tries to use some emotive buzz words, but it seems mostly to be in an effort to cover up the fact that she can't think of a tactful or sensible answer.

The Only Way is Essex

This transcript features two girls chatting about a date that one of them has recently been on. It encourages students to examine the function of 'like', commonly thought of as a superfluous filler.

Activity 2

a Lydia uses the word 'like' nine times and Danni uses it three times.

b Students may have a range of ideas. The following are valid possibilities:

- Lydia says more in this interaction as she is the one sharing the story, so there are more opportunities for her to use this word.
- Lydia may have got into the habit of using this word more than Danni – it is a stronger feature of her idiolect (personal way of speaking).
- Lydia may be a bit embarrassed about describing the date so she uses 'like' to fill the gaps or to be vague in her descriptions.

c The differences between the uses of 'like' are quite subtle and students will need to have looked closely at each utterance in the context of the transcript to accurately match the examples and explanations as follows:

Example	Explanation of how 'like' is used
1 'you get like all excited'	D Used to give some extra emphasis to the description that comes afterwards.
2 'your belly goes round like a washing machine'	E Used to make a direct comparison between two things.
3 'you're like [looks up to the sky and waves head side to side] ah in the clouds'	A Used to introduce an impersonation of someone else.
4 'like a little kiss'	B Used to show something is similar, but not *exactly* the same.
5 'like (.) like'	C Used instead of 'erm', hesitating about how to respond.

Reality talent show

This is a transcript of a piece to camera by two contestants as they wait behind the scenes of *Britain's Got Talent*.

Activity 3

a

Jonathan's speech	What is he talking about?	How fluently does he speak? Are there any pauses or fillers or other features that disrupt the flow or meaning of his speech?
First utterance	He is recalling his experiences of school, particularly being bullied.	He uses lots of fillers like 'sort of' and 'like'. He has a false start: 'I'd just (1) it'd just'. He sometimes repeats words 'it it', 'when when'. Pauses get longer the more he talks.
Second utterance	He is talking about his friendship with Charlotte.	Few pauses. No other non-fluency features.

b The sentence starters provided should encourage students to make a clear link between Jonathan's emotions and the fluency of his speech. When he talks about something that caused him pain, his speech becomes more broken and tentative, as though he feels uncomfortable or is reliving those memories. However, when talking about something positive, Charlotte's friendship and her effect on his confidence, this is reflected in a more assured and fluent speech style.

c Charlotte does use non-fluency features, but the content of what she is saying suggests she is more assertive.

- She re-words 'I wouldn't sit' to 'I couldn't sit there with my mouth shut' which shows her determination to speak out and stand up for her friend.
- The phrase 'mouth shut' sounds quite blunt and direct, perhaps showing she is that kind of character too.
- She words her opinions strongly to give them more force: 'you really need to get to know them'.
- She repeats herself when she says 'you've got you've got to'; although this may be an accidental false start, it emphasises the insistent language she is using.

Second thoughts

A job interview

This is a transcript of part of an interview. Annie, the restaurant manager, is interviewing John for a part-time job as a waiter.

Activity 1

a Ranking of reasons for John's false start could vary. However, given that he goes on to answer this first question quite fully, in an organised way with relatively few other non-fluency features, the following ranking seems most likely:

   i He is nervous about the interview.

   ii He needs a little more time to form a good answer.

   iii He does not understand the question.

b There are two other false starts: 'it's form. well really smart' and 'the the staff'.

c 'it's form. well really smart' – here, John is about to use the word formal again but appears to stop himself halfway through. This may be because Annie has just asked him to explain his previous use of this word. He may think she doesn't like his word choice so he avoids using it again or he may just realise he can't use the word 'formal' to explain what 'formal' means!

'the the staff' – again, this false start seems to be as a result of Annie's input. Just before the repetition of this word, Annie overlaps his words, saying 'mhmm' to show she is following what is being said. While Annie is being supportive, this appears to momentarily put John off his stride, upsetting the fluency ever so slightly.

Mother and daughter interaction

This is a transcript of an interaction between two women. Debbie is helping her mother Joan to fit her hearing aid.

Activity 2

a Two false starts from Joan. Two false starts from Debbie. Four false starts in the first two utterances.

b The key point here is that students recognise the physical situation and activity that is accompanying the interaction. Students should explain that, because Debbie is fitting the hearing aid, she is probably concentrating quite hard on what she is doing; Joan may also be experiencing some discomfort as a result. This will distract them both from what they are saying.

c There is room for debate regarding this answer.

Some students may agree that being silent is preferable: the running commentary could annoy Joan; Debbie actually sounds a bit mean in the way she keeps ordering Joan to keep still; Joan might not be able to hear the many instructions Debbie gives her; Debbie might do a better job of fitting the device if she wasn't talking the whole time.

However, hopefully students will also acknowledge that silence in this situation could be quite disconcerting: Joan will not be able to tell if her hearing aid works; depending on Joan's level of hearing, Debbie can give her mum instructions that might help with the fitting of the hearing aid; Debbie can reassure her mum about what she is doing.

Plenary activity

This task could be extended to think about the effects of silence generally. What does silence represent in interaction? When might silence be used for a particular effect? Who is likely to use silence in this way? Students should be able to draw on a variety of experiences to explore ideas of silence linked to respect and listening, anger and tension, expectation and power.

Depending on the nature of the class and your own teaching style, you could experiment with and model silence yourself. Perhaps use it to get the group quiet, or in response to a pupil's contribution. Discuss the meaning of such silence and the different reactions it can generate. Alternatively, simply suggest these examples as starting points for discussion.

Going to dinner

In this transcript Anisha and Naomi discuss Naomi's outfit choice. They are about to go out for the evening. Anisha has been waiting for Naomi to get ready.

GCSE Spoken Language Skills
Section A: Spoken language skills

Activity 3

a There are many examples of Anisha's non-fluency. Four possible examples are shown below. Accept any valid descriptions and explanations of examples.

Examples of non-fluency features in Anisha's speech	Description of how Anisha loses fluency and why you think this might have happened
A: no I didn't mean erm it is a nice dress	Anisha starts to defend herself and then hesitates with a voiced pause and does not finish the original sentence. It seems she decides to change strategy and says something positive instead by complimenting the dress. She might be trying to avoid having an argument.
A: //no// //no no//	Anisha overlaps Naomi, to try to interrupt her with the first 'no', but Naomi will not allow her to. Anisha has to repeat herself to emphasise that she did not mean anything rude.
A: well the skirt bit is quite you know a bit big (.) puffy	There are some vague fillers here like 'well' and 'you know', as though Anisha is now trying to be more tentative in what she's saying. She also repairs 'quite' to 'a bit' to try to play down the size of the skirt. She even repairs 'big' to 'puffy', perhaps realising that Naomi might take the word 'big' more personally.
A: well you look quite you (.) you look quite …	Anisha makes quite a lengthy false start and it seems like she is trying to gain some time to find the right word to describe how Naomi looks. She realises Naomi is being sensitive to her comments so she is searching for a word that sounds positive but which still gets her point across that she thinks Naomi's outfit is too formal for the occasion ('dressed up').

b Students may find fault with Anisha because of her impatience and abrupt language use at the beginning of the interaction. Her questioning utterance 'are you really wearing that' is insensitive as it suggests disbelief and calling the dress 'that' makes her sound quite disdainful of it. She tends to choose words that could be easily misinterpreted, like 'annoying' and 'big'. She also perseveres with her criticism even when it is clear that Naomi does not see the formality of her outfit as a problem.

Students may also find fault with Naomi for her increasing sensitivity to Anisha's comments. She puts words in her mouth: 'I just look horrible in it' and she makes sarcastic comments like 'big and puffy (.) ok (.) thanks'. She questions most things Anisha says, e.g. 'what do you mean annoying', repeating words she sees as being insulting, which makes her sound confrontational. She doesn't seem to notice that Anisha is trying to adapt her language (even if unsuccessfully) to try to be more sensitive.

c The scripts students create should hopefully generate a more tactful and measured version of this interaction.

Plenary activity

The task could be extended by asking students to annotate their scripts to explain how they crafted the language of the participants to show more tact, politeness, or sensitivity.

Whose turn is it anyway?

The Jonas Brothers

This transcript features an American band consisting of three brothers who, in this interaction, were in their late teens and early twenties. They recount an incident at one of their gigs the night before.

Activity 1

a i   The reading activity is made difficult by the amount of overlapping and low frequency of pauses. Those students who master it could also read aloud to the class.

   ii The tone is best described as 'lively' or possibly 'friendly'.

b Fans may have found it confusing to listen to given that they overlap one another so much. As this was broadcast online the brothers may have had a global audience, so non-native English speakers may have found it hard to follow the pace of their speech.

c Accept any sensible selections of clarifying/supporting overlaps. Some examples are shown below:

Clarifying overlaps

Nick: //it wasn't out// of anger or// anything

Joe: //he was trying to give Nick a nice pair of yellow// sunglasses

Supporting overlaps

Nick: //oh yeah oh yeah//

Nick: //this is what// happened

Joe: //waah waah awesome//

Kevin: //oh no//

Joe: //amazing//

Nick: //it was// it was pretty crazy

Plenary activity

It may be worth noting that the majority of these overlaps come from Joe and Nick. What does this reveal about the roles of the brothers in this particular context?

Speaking and listening

Secret linguistic study: this task could act as a starter activity before examining the committee meeting transcript.

Organise the class into groups of about five. The aim is to provoke a discussion in the group on any topic. One possibility could be for groups to discuss and devise a 'Dream Teachers' Team'. They need to agree on five celebrity/historical figures to take over the running of the school.

Select one person from each group to act as a 'silent observer'. Give these people a secret set of instructions asking them to keep a record of the others' speech. You could provide a table such as the following for the silent observer to record their observations.

Name	Interrupts someone	Changes subject	Agrees with someone	Disagrees with someone

Following five minutes of observed discussion, explain the truth of the task. Ask observers to feed back the roles of people in the group or patterns they noticed.

A committee meeting

This transcript of part of a committee meeting features five participants, each of whom has a slightly different purpose, role and style in the interaction. It may be worth clarifying the format of official meetings beforehand: agenda items, making motions, seconding motions, etc.

Activity 2

a

	Number of times this person speaks	Number of times this person starts speaking when someone else is speaking	Number of times this person gets talked over by someone else before they have finished
Mr Bhatt	9	1	4
Ms Martin	3	0	2
Mr Wilson	3	2	0
Ms Hewitt	9	4	1
Ms Olson	1	0	0

b Strong arguments can be made for the power/status of both Mr Bhatt and Ms Hewitt.

Mr Bhatt – takes the most turns, he seems to be chairing the meeting; he introduces topics; he reminds people of rules and procedures; he takes a firm tone 'I **understand** Ms Hewitt'; he is shown some respect by Ms Hewitt in the form of an apology.

Ms Hewitt – takes the same number of turns as Mr Bhatt; she interrupts people frequently; she speaks for others 'no one wants to discuss this'; she repeats her points to give them more force; she questions the chair (Mr Bhatt) in quite a casual way 'how long are you gonna wait'; her motion ultimately moves the discussion on.

c A range of possibilities might be suggested: interrupt them back so they know how it feels; carry on talking when the person tries to interrupt; let them speak and then come back to your original point; explicitly say, 'let me finish', 'you can talk in a second'; tell the person once outside the situation that they are interrupting others too much and it seems rude.

The personality and status of the individual, your relationship with them and the precise situation will probably determine which method is best.

A family breakfast

This transcript is of a breakfast-time interaction between a mother, father and their 12-year-old daughter Katie. Their baby son, Tom, is also present. The sequencing of utterances makes this a more challenging transcript to follow.

Activity 3

a

Who ...	Talking to ...	About ...
Mother	Tom	The breakfast she is feeding him.
Father	Katie	School/science.
Father	Mother	What time train/bus she is getting.
Mother	Katie	School/science.
Father	Tom	Says his name, comments on mess.

b Four out of five of Katie's utterances are followed by her mother or father talking to each other or to Tom. They do not immediately respond to what she has said.

c If students have correctly identified the previous pattern, they should suggest Katie will be feeling frustrated, irritated, overlooked and less important.

Speaking and listening

The study of spoken language is a relatively new part of GCSE courses and it should give your students some very beneficial knowledge and skills. Get students working with a partner and discussing how they could use their understanding of spoken interaction in other areas of English study. Ask them if there could there be any other real-life or practical ways that their knowledge of spoken language might come in useful.

Check your learning

A model answer

When the teacher calls Daniel over to explain himself, his first utterance starts with filler words 'yeah well'. This is probably because he is trying to think up a good excuse as he knows she feels sad about his actions and he will be in trouble if he can't explain. As he gives his excuse, there is a voiced pause 'I was erm only playing' which may hint that he is uncomfortable and telling a lie.

The teacher has a false start when she says 'but what on (.) what what were you doing'. This could simply be a mistake, or it may be she was about to say 'what on earth' but decided that this might not be appropriate when talking to a four-year-old so she repairs her word choice.

Daniel overlaps his teacher a couple of times in the interaction, for example when he says 'I didn't know'. He may be eager to give his excuses so he overlaps before his teacher has finished speaking. It may also be that, because he is so young, he is not aware that this could be seen as rude by his teacher.

Finally, Daniel admits what he did, but there is a false start in his utterance: 'I (1) I hit it on that wall'. It seems as though he might have been going to give another excuse but the longer pause suggests he has second thoughts about lying or cannot think of a better excuse so he tells the truth.

2 Interaction and the structure of talk: Following the rules

AO focus

AO2:

- Understand variations in spoken language, explaining why language changes in relation to contexts.
- Evaluate the impact of spoken language choices in their own and others' use.

In this unit your students will:

- learn how conversations conform to unwritten rules
- understand how speakers use language to maintain interest and keep conversations fluent.

Key terms

Key terms the students are introduced to in this unit:

- Hyperbole
- Cue
- Phatic communication
- Transactional and interactional talk
- Back-channelling
- Latching on (=)
- Metaphor
- Interrogative
- Adjective

Transcripts included in this unit

A Kiss FM radio interview: Tulisa speaks about her new album *Young*

Starting and finishing: snippets of conversation showing the use of cues. *The Only Way is Essex*: a conversation showing the use of phatic communication subtext

A telephone conversation: two lovers saying goodnight

Transactional or interactional? Conversations in a greengrocer's/at home/in the canteen

An interactional conversation: two girls discussing their websites

talkSPORT radio phone-in show: how presenters use language to involve their listeners

Back-channelling: a lack of feedback

Back-channelling: examples

A job interview: back-channelling and its purpose in maintaining interest in conversations

A sportsman on a chat show discussing a footballing injury.

Oleanna: extracts from the play

See pp63–71 for photocopiable versions of these transcripts for students to work on.

Getting started

The purpose of this unit is to introduce students to how spontaneous conversations often follow a set of 'unwritten rules'. The opening transcript between Tulisa and Clara from Kiss FM is intended to illustrate how cooperative conversations are structured and introduces some terminology and concepts that students can refer back to in their own study. This type of annotation can be used as a model generally when studying transcripts in the classroom.

The first three activities offer students the chance to think about their own daily interactions and to question why people generally respond in a similar way to each other. It is fun to encourage students to build on their own experiences; they may identify situations that they have found awkward because people didn't respond as expected.

Although some activities suggest rewriting the script, it may be more useful to role play these sort of transactions. You can then encourage students to record the formulaic utterances and responses that they use.

Opening and closing cues

Starting and finishing

This section introduces the idea of phatic communication and its purpose.

Activity 1

a As a starter, give students a line that they have to say to each other which would inevitably end in phatic communication. Cards that say things like 'How are you?' or 'What have you been up to?' or even just 'All right' could be given out to pairs. Students can then go on to complete the table in the activity.

b Most pairs in the class will have answered in exactly the same way. This short introductory

GCSE Spoken Language Skills
Section A: Spoken language skills

activity builds on the idea of opening patterns, but also gets students to recognise the social value of phatic communication and to reflect on how difficult conversations would be without it.

c By rewriting an ending to Text B, where character A is asking for change, students could use closing sequences such as, 'thanks I really appreciate it' or 'don't worry, thanks anyway', which show their awareness of stock phrases used in particular circumstances.

The Only Way is Essex

This transcript explores how the type of phatic communication used can indicate the tone of the conversation.

Activity 2

a Students should identify phrases such as 'how you doin'', 'good thanks you' and 'how you getting on' as examples of phatic communication.

b By matching statements and examples, students can decide how the phatic communication suggests tone.
   i   Mark finds Sam attractive = 'you look nice'
   ii Sam has something on her mind = 'not bad' (the minimal answer suggests reticence)
   iii The couple are alone = any of Mark's compliments

c The script task is a chance for students to draw on their knowledge of phatic communication and to be creative. Encourage students to think of examples of good or bad news before writing.

You put the phone down!

This transcript looks at closing cues in general and telephone conversations in particular.

Activity 3

As a starter, you could ask students to think of someone who they have to talk to but whom they are keen to get away from. Ask them to think about how they try to end conversations and question why they avoid being blunt (if, indeed, they do!).

a The purpose of the conversation is to show that both participants are eager to convey their love for each other and to express how they wish they could be together.

b This activity allows students to identify adjacent pairs, as well as exploring the way in which people imply meanings. Using the table, students can see how many of the pairs mimic each other.

Woman	Man
Bye	Bye darling
Press the button	Going to press the button
Night	Night
Love you	Adore you

c In the rewrite, look for students using polite closing cues such as 'it's getting late' or 'so, I'll speak to you tomorrow' to show W's desire to finish the conversation. With M, students should use some questions or topic shifts as an attempt to prolong the conversation. Phrases such as 'what time did you get to sleep last night?' or 'what are you doing tomorrow?' ensure that W has to answer.

Stretch yourself

As part of a plenary, you could ask students to think of examples of spoken English that follow relatively strict patterns. They should come up with a range of contexts that build on the work in the unit. Although they may start with things like opening and closings of conversations, they will probably apply the work to situations such as buying a bus/train ticket, calling a helpline for information or responding to bad news.

Where am I? Transactional, interactional and context

The question of context is a key one that is important across all of the units. The aim in this unit is to get students to acknowledge that different contexts affect their language, its structures and formality.

Transactional or interactional?

This transcript introduces transactional conversations (ones that have a specific purpose) and interactional conversations (ones that do not have a specific purpose).

Activity 1

The terms 'transactional' and 'interactional' are useful in helping students to make an initial decision about why the conversation is taking place. However, you must stress that transactional conversations can easily become interactional, as the 'greengrocer' snippet aims to illustrate.

a The topic of each conversation:
   Text 1 = the weather
   Text 2 = television
   Text 3 = directions

b Type of conversation:

Text 1 = interactional

Text 2 = transactional

Text 3 = transactional

c The purpose of each conversation:

Text 1 = to be friendly

Text 2 = to get own way over television choice

Text 3 = directions

School website

This transcript helps students to see how turn-taking can also be linked to concepts such as dominance and control.

Activity 2

a The initial topic of the conversation is websites that the girls have made at school.

b In order to answer this question, ask students to consider their friendship groups and to discuss how their conversations are often about bonding and enjoyment and are, therefore, interactional.

c In answer to this question, get students to identify that although the topic is 'websites that they have made at school', the purpose is to enjoy each other's company by teasing each other and reminiscing about a shared moment.

talkSPORT radio phone-in show

This transcript takes a similar idea but shows how the purpose of a conversation in this case is about making the audience interested and excited. Here, students can draw on their literary knowledge and apply terms such as 'metaphor' to the spoken text.

Activity 3

a Encourage students to see how the concept of an imaginary Sports Bar creates a virtual place for listeners to imagine the conversation, which will in turn make them feel invited to phone in and add their views.

Welcome to the Sports Bar	Phatic communication
Would you have him at your club?	Interrogative sentences
Taking your calls	Direct address

b The idea of Sam Delaney being Jason Cundy's 'wingman' should foster discussion about the intended audience and, in particular, the traditionally male representation of sport radio in general.

c Discussing grammatical usage is covered in detail in other units (Unit 4 Grammar and structure and Unit 5 Planned and unplanned speech), but it is useful to highlight here to students that these inclusive pronouns are a pattern that we both expect and accept.

Pronoun and term	Effect
'me' Jason Cundy: first-person pronoun	Making it clear to the audience who is talking.
'we'll be discussing': first-person plural pronoun	Showing the audience that their views are a part of the show.
'we broke the news last night': first-person plural pronoun	Speaking on behalf of Talk Sport and emphasising how they are the first to find out sports news.
'taking your calls': second-person pronoun	To involve the readers and encourage them to phone in.

Maintaining interest

The main focus in this section is to identify turn-taking strategies that encourage and extend conversations. The key term 'back-channelling' is introduced as a useful way of describing the sounds and words that people use to signal that they are listening. We also look at how people choose language to show that they want to hear more and, again, how the context of the conversation may require this more than other discussions.

Speaking and listening

As a starter, you could role play a situation where selected students are told to give no response at all to an anecdote told to them by a partner. (The anecdote could be anything – a funny story of what happened to them on holiday etc.) As a class, discuss how the lack of feedback made the students feel.

Depending on the class, you could do this as a prearranged activity with a student prepared to perform or give pairs written instructions.

The following three activities are intended to get students to draw on their own experiences to think about why back-channelling is a necessary part of everyday talk.

Back-channelling: a lack of feedback

This transcript explores the impact of limited back-channelling.

Activity 1

a Your students could give a number of responses to this activity. Adjectives such as 'short', 'blunt', 'abrupt', etc. are along the right track.

GCSE Spoken Language Skills
Section A: Spoken language skills

b A rewrite could look like this:

A: how's your mum and dad

B: they're really well thanks. In fact they're on holiday at the moment

A: is your mum still working (.) at the post office

B: not any more, she works in Asda now and enjoys it much more actually

A: oh (.) when did she leave?

B: I think it was a few months ago now. And where are you working now?

c Students will have probably used politeness markers such as 'thanks' to make the conversation sound more cooperative. They may have asked questions to extend the conversation.

Back-channelling: examples

This transcript shows the importance of back-channelling in social and interactional conversations.

Activity 2

a Examples of back-channelling in the transcript are: '(laughs)', 'two weeks', 'god two weeks', 'really?'

b If a student chose, for example, 'two weeks', they should be able to recognise that H understands the dramatic impact of the short amount of time between getting a tattoo and then breaking up. The use of 'really?' at the end of the conversation is an attempt to encourage C to carry on with the story, even though her previous utterance 'and then it was like (.) I can't believe it' is a bit vague.

c The table that lists different types of audiences and the back-channelling that you might use is another attempt to focus on how context is an integral part of the language that we choose to use. Students tend to enjoy this activity and can readily relate to how the use of back-channelling to be polite is very different to the back-channelling they use to encourage gossip or the retelling of an entertaining story.

Context	Back-channel word or phrase	Effect on conversation
Phone call to grandparent	Oh goodness	Politely shows that grandchild is listening.
Talking to a friend about another friend's behaviour	No way!	Encourages the gossip and shows interest.
Listening to a very long and boring story	mmmm	Shows that you are listening but that you are not encouraging more detail.

Speaking and listening

The following two interviews are intended to show how particular genres of spoken English rely on back-channelling in order to work. Interviews are a good source of study for interaction.

As a starter, you might like students to think of the different types of interviews that they are aware of and how the language would differ depending on context.

Most classes will come up with a comprehensive variety:

- chat shows
- radio interviews
- news interviews
- sports pundits
- police interviews
- job interviews
- college or careers interviews.

You could ask students to think about how the back-channelling would vary according to context. Studying the job interview and the chat show interview should allow students to identify features of supportive behaviour and to explore the differences between the two genres.

A job interview

This transcript explores back-channelling and its purpose in maintaining interest in conversations.

Activity 3

a The director wants to make the interviewee feel comfortable, which should encourage them to expand on their personal qualities and suitability for the job.

b The director back-channels a lot and students should identify 'yeah', 'yep yep', 'yeah absolutely very', 'OK mm hmm', 'right OK', 'yeah yeah, oh absolutely'.

c A model answer: the director uses back-channelling at the beginning of the conversation to encourage the interviewee to carry on talking about the research that they had done before the interview. The use of 'yeah' has the required effect and the interviewee is quickly able to link their research to the job they have applied for.

Stretch yourself

Sportsman on a chat show

This transcript shows the participants' use of latching on to maintain the live and television audience's interest.

a   Examples of words and phrases that Jake uses are: 'actually completely tore', 'wow', 'it truly was the experience'.

b   Words that are repeated in the conversation are, 'injury', 'tore/torn', 'Achilles tendon', 'burning' and they create a graphic description of Daniel's injury.

c   The use of onomatopoeic words such as 'rip' and the imagery of 'on fire' and 'burning in my thigh spreading all down my leg' create a dramatic account of the injury.

But … don't interrupt!

The last section of this unit focuses on the ways in which turn-taking can also show conflict and disapproval.

Speaking and listening

As a starter, ask the whole class how they might show disapproval, regardless of context. Students usually come up with a long list of strategies such as: minimal responses, interruptions, body language, looking at their phone, avoiding eye contact, turning away, looking away, changing the topic, changing their tone of voice, sarcasm and language choices (swearing or more formality). You could then discuss how different contexts probably demand different strategies. Give students a list of situations to consider:

- parent in a shop
- sibling at home
- employer at work
- vague acquaintance at college in class
- close friend on the bus
- teacher at staffroom door.

Oleanna

The *Oleanna* activities are designed to encourage students to explore how playwrights draw on spoken language in order to create believable characters and also dramatic tension.

The *Oleanna* activities elicit an understanding that Carol is behaving differently from accepted norms. The way in which she changes subject is different from the transcripts that students will have looked at earlier.

Activity 1

a   Encourage students to discuss why this quite awkward interaction has been constructed as such. They should also draw on their knowledge of context to recognise that Carol and John aren't behaving in the way their roles usually expect.

Lines used to change the topic are all from Carol and students should identify:

'You're buying a new house.'

'Because of your promotion.'

'Why did you stay here with me?'

'Why?'

'You said "everyone has problems."'

b   As shown above, Carol is the person who always changes the topic.

c   Students will probably identify Carol's direct questioning style as being blunt, unfriendly and serious.

Activity 2

a   Students should produce a list with the following results.

Carol: 'Stay here'	John: 'Stay here'
John: 'I like you'	Carol: 'You like me'
Carol: 'Why?'	John: 'Why? Well?'
Carol: 'You said "everyone has problems."'	John: 'Everyone has problems.'

b   The conversation style is certainly unusual and by pulling out specific examples of mirroring, students should be able to make suggestions about Mamet's intentions. The table gives students some interpretations to agree or disagree with, but they may have some of their own interpretations to add.

c   The final extract encourages students to explore how John's language suggests that he wants to extricate himself from the conversation. The way in which he interrupts Carol and stops patterning her questions means that he has lost patience to some extent. Carol's shorter and more direct questions and statements show that she has a problem with how John has spoken to her.

Check your learning

This activity is difficult and asks students to not only role play but to adopt a sophisticated style while they do this. They should role play first and then write a similar script. The script doesn't have to be exactly like the role play, but would have drawn on its structures. The activity is most effective when students write down and identify examples of interruptions and overlaps because this allows them to recognise that interruptions are not always competitive and that, in the case of John, repeating or overlapping is a sign of weakness.

3 Lexis: The words we use

AO focus

AO2:

- Understand variations in spoken language, explaining why language changes in relation to contexts.
- Evaluate the impact of spoken language choices in their own and others' use.

In this unit your students will:

- learn to identify and describe the different sorts of words typical of certain contexts
- learn the way in which a speaker's knowledge, background, purpose, attitude and relationship with the person they're talking to can influence their choices of vocabulary
- focus on jargon, slang and emotive language use
- consider and evaluate the range of effects such lexical choices can have on the listener.

Key terms

Key terms the students are introduced to in this unit:

- Lexis
- Informal
- Subject-specific
- Jargon
- Connotations
- Colloquial
- Formal
- Register
- Slang
- Emotive
- Denotation
- Implied meaning

Transcripts included in this unit

At the hairdressers: hair stylist consulting with a new client

A science lecture: an expert on a specialist subject

Kes: delivering a presentation to the class

Business interview: jargon under pressure

Radio broadcast: DJs using modern slang

Our Day Out: troublesome students on the bus

The Wild One: slang from another time

Music award ceremony: enthusiastic responses

Hugh Grant at the Press Standards Enquiry: expressing concern

Football discussion: emphasising ideas

See pp72–77 for photocopiable versions of these transcripts for students to work on.

Getting started

The worked example at the beginning of the unit looks at language in a very specific situation: a consultation between a hairstylist and his client. In this situation the stylist uses an informal register and inclusive tone to try to set the client at ease, but also takes control, demonstrating his knowledge of hairdressing through subject-specific language. The client seems a little hesitant in her initial responses, but is either subdued or reassured into agreement by the confident tone and positive description offered by the stylist. The annotations demonstrate how key terms can be worked into analytical comments about the participants' language choices.

Review and reflect

As part of a plenary activity, you could ask your students to read the transcript, again pointing out that it seems as though the hairstylist manages to reassure the client through their word choices. Get your students to write a short script (10–15 lines) in which a patient goes to see their doctor about their sore throat. Remember, the doctor will want to reassure their patient.

When they have finished, get them to look back over their script and annotate their own work, labelling any specific types of words that they think they have used to suit the context.

Getting technical

Speaking and listening

Personal jargon

This paired activity could take the form of an interview. Students question one another about their hobbies/interests/favourite subjects, asking for detailed descriptions of what they have to do to participate in this hobby/interest. They could jot

Unit 3 Lexis: The words we use

down any word that their partner says that they think could be classed as jargon.

Alternatively, they could devise a script for an instructional video in which they introduce the audience to a new activity or hobby, using and explaining the jargon words as they go. Their ability to deliver this effectively could be assessed by the rest of the class using the 'Communicating and adapting language' assessment criteria for Speaking and listening in your GCSE specification.

Science lecture to GCSE students

Professor Brian Cox addresses an audience of Year 11 students. Two transcribed samples are used: one from the beginning of the lecture and one from later on.

Activity 1

a Words connected to the field of science might include: science, moon, earth, magnetic field, universe, Big Bang, northern lights, isotope(s), elements, carbon, protons, neutrons, carbon-12, oxygen, solar system, planets, sun, carbon-14.

It may be worth noting during the discussion that some of these words belong to more than one field.

b ii They need specialist words to talk about their subject precisely.

This is the most likely reason, but it may be worth exploring the alternatives. Can students think of real people or characters who seem to use this kind of language to intimidate others?

c Any valid answer such as: the professor uses less specialist language at the beginning of the lecture than he does later on to give the students time to settle into the lecture. This avoids overwhelming and intimidating them early on and the speaker can focus on being friendly and accessible to get them engaged in the topic.

Kes: Billy's presentation

A scripted extract from Barry Hines' play in which Billy, the central character, is asked to do a presentation to the class, explaining his new hobby (falcon training).

Activity 2

a i As well as 'jesses', Billy uses: 'swivel', 'leash', 'bating'.

   ii Billy is either asked to explain what the word means or he volunteers an explanation himself without prompting.

b Any valid answer that recognises that the audience does not necessarily share Billy's knowledge and will not understand his references without further explanation.

c Accept valid answers that consider any of the following:

Advantages:
- Billy can be really specific as he explains the process of training.
- Mr Farthing and Billy's classmates may be impressed by his knowledge of these technical terms and respect him for being an expert.
- Mr Farthing may be pleased that Billy has the ability to explain terms so clearly and that he begins to do this without being asked.

Disadvantages:
- Billy could alienate his classmates as they may get frustrated by the specialist language or think that Billy is showing off.

An interview with the bank manager

This is a transcript of a meeting in which the bank manager presses Owen for answers regarding his business proposal. In a bid to gain a business loan, Owen attempts to persuade his bank manager that his business idea is a viable one.

Activity 3

a Owen knows he has not done what the bank manager expects him to have done (his market research), so he tries to avoid answering the question in the hope that the conversation will move on to a different topic.

b Accept valid answers that might include the following or similar:

Describe the tactic he uses and give an example	Explain what you think he hopes the effect will be
He uses several long, complex words, e.g. 'correspondence', 'labour-intensive', 'properties'.	He hopes these word choices will make him sound more intelligent and that the bank manager will take him more seriously.
He uses jargon that relates to business, e.g. 'demographic', 'uptake', 'e-subscription', 'target consumer', 'unique selling point'.	He probably hopes this gives the impression that he is experienced in this field and should therefore be trusted to run a business.
He uses positive language, e.g. 'strong', 'very high', 'even better'.	He wants to promote the positives of his idea in the hope that these may distract the bank manager from his question about market research.

13

GCSE Spoken Language Skills
Section A: Spoken language skills

Describe the tactic he uses and give an example	Explain what you think he hopes the effect will be
He keeps talking even when Mike interrupts with another question: 'on //a national scale// the demand for e-subscription will be even better'.	As above, he may think if he ignores the question and finishes his positive point, the question will be forgotten.
He answers the question in an indirect way: 'the proposal has been informed by my partner'.	He hopes that the bank manager will see this as a form of research and be satisfied by this as an answer.
He avoids saying no, e.g. 'not for this particular service'.	He doesn't seem to want to admit defeat here; he might be trying to suggest to the bank manager that he has done lots of market research for other projects and, therefore, it won't be a problem.

c Responses to this task are likely to vary so reasonable evaluations of language should be rewarded.

Students' responses may commend the enthusiasm and perseverance of Owen, as well as his ability to use some complex structures, specialist business jargon and maintain a positive tone.

However, more sophisticated responses may criticise Owen's evasive answers and lack of specific detail, noting that he tends to use complex but often empty language to misdirect the bank manager or disguise the truth.

Street talk

Speaking and listening

Personal jargon

Colloquial:
- 'Hey, how you doing?'
- 'We had a great time on our hols.'

Jargon:
- 'We need to set out the foundations along the line of the boundary.'
- 'We'll be teeing off for a par 4 but take into account the dog-leg on the right.'

Slang:
- 'That sucks, you must be hacked off.'
- 'The film was wicked man, you should try to catch it.'

Radio DJ webcast

This is a transcript of two London-based DJs who, in this example, dissect the fashions of celebrity figures using a range of non-standard lexical forms.

Activity 1

a Ac, Be, Cd, Dg, Ef, Fh, Ga, Hb.

b Swagalicious: students should be able to deduce from the context of its use that this means fashionable/smart/attractive, and recognise that this is a blended word made from the words 'swag' and 'delicious', hence the positive connotations.

c Accept any valid (or vaguely recognisable!) answers based on students' own experiences.

Stretch yourself

The data collection for the investigative task relating to slang could be set for homework. Students could use the list of words from the preceding activity or another list devised through discussion in class as the basis for their questionnaires.

Results could be collated as a whole class and results presented in graph form (cross-curricular links).

Our Day Out

This is a scripted extract from Willy Russell's play in which secondary-school students are travelling by bus to the school trip destination. The 'naughty' students plan to smoke at the back of the bus.

Activity 2

a

	Digga	Reilly	Little Kid
The victim			✓
The accomplice	✓		
The goody two shoes			✓
The bully		✓	
The sneak			✓
The bad boy		✓	

b

Slang	Explain what this choice of language shows about the character
Digga: 'I'll keep Dixie.'	Digga is willing to keep watch for Reilly. Maybe he is just being a good friend, or he might be too scared of getting caught himself to take the lead.
Reilly: 'open that friggin' window.'	Reilly is giving an order. It shows he believes he is in charge and can tell people what to do. The use of the slang word 'friggin' gives it extra force and makes him sound more impatient and aggressive.
Reilly: 'I'll gob y''	Reilly is making a threat of violence. There will be consequences if he is not obeyed. Again, this suggests he is a bully and used to getting his own way.

Unit 3 Lexis: The words we use

c Accept any valid answers including those that consider situations where slang is used to:
- build relationships and bonds within close-knit groups
- create an informal and friendly tone
- exclude people or hide information from them (for whatever reason!).

The Wild One

This transcript is of a clip from the 1950s film starring Marlon Brando. It is peppered with American slang of the era.

Activity 3

a Students should be able to identify the negative connotations in Johnny's criticism that Kathie is 'too square' or in his comment that her suggestion is 'cornball style'. They should be able to interpret meaning sufficiently to explain that Johnnie thinks Kathie is too proper, naïve, boring or 'un-cool'.

b The order below is a suggestion only. There is no 'correct' ranking. However, it is hoped that discussion should reveal that students have considered the following:
  (1) He is in a motorcycle gang – the gang may have developed code words for things to keep outsiders excluded.
  (2) He is trying to impress Kathie – he wants Kathie to see him as a rebel. Therefore, if he uses language that most people don't know or understand, Kathie may see him as more interesting.
  (3) He is a young man – he may see using slang as more macho and tough.
  (4) They are in a café – there may be an audience here and Johnny wants to show how different he is from those around him.
  (5) He has got into the habit of using slang – it isn't unusual for people to pick up words and say them without even thinking, so this is possible too.
  (6) He is from out of town – if these were dialect slang words, then this could be possible, especially if Johnnie's hometown does not have much contact with Kathie's town.

c Accept paragraphs that follow the suggested structure and explore ideas such as those listed above, using appropriate evidence.

Loaded words

Music award ceremony

This is a transcript of a red-carpet interview in which a music artist talks with enthusiasm about his love of music.

Activity 1

a He feels enthusiastic, motivated and very positive about making music. It's the focus of his life.

b Accept the selection of all or part of the following utterances:
- 'gave me like a a passion a dream a hunger something to really live for'
- 'discovering music and falling in love with it made me realise that (.) I had a purpose'

c Triple: 'a passion a dream a hunger' or 'I had a purpose I had something that I wanted to do and I had something that I had to work my butt off to achieve'.

Speaking and listening

Connotation v. denotation

This could be a paired or small group activity. Groups could mind-map the connotations of each word on to a large sheet of paper. These idea-sheets can be stuck to the board or wall for comparison and whole-class discussion.

As an extension, groups could generate their own word lists after being given an initiating word, e.g. 'male', 'female', 'police officer', 'home', 'leader'. It is important to emphasise that they are aiming to find words with a range of connotations, not just negative ones! Ideas can be presented and explained by the group.

Hugh Grant at the Press Standards Inquiry

This is a transcript from the 2012 inquiry in which the actor gives his personal and negative opinion of the British Press.

Activity 2

a Toxic – denotes poisonous but suggests that the press is capable of causing great pain or discomfort; Hugh Grant wants to present the press as being extremely unpleasant and dangerous and causing great trauma to the people whose lives they disrupt.

GCSE Spoken Language Skills
Section A: Spoken language skills

b Accept valid answers such as the following:

Short quote where emotive language is used	How are we supposed to feel?
'main tactic being bullying and intimidation and blackmail'	Angry that the press does what it does, causing suffering to its victims.
'this country has had historically a good record standing up to bullies'	Proud of our country and its high moral standards and sense of right and wrong.
'it's time that this country found the courage to stand up to this bully now'	Motivated to join the fight against the press.

c Changing his wording here hints that there are people who are responsible for the press's bad behaviour. It suggests a higher authority that has given permission in the past but that also has the power to stop the press behaving in this way.

Football discussion

This transcript features a discussion between regular panellists on a televised programme about football. The men describe and pass comment on an unusual incident involving Premier League player Ashley Cole.

Activity 3

a The options provided should promote a variety of responses, though there are disadvantages to each.
- 'hit a student' – maintains the short, sharp sound of 'shot' but the meaning is ambiguous (it is not clear that he injured the student by aiming at him and pulling the trigger).
- 'popped a cap in a student' – sounds very informal; this kind of slang would only sound convincing from people of a certain age or background and, even then, it is unlikely to suit the serious tone of the discussion taking place here; middle-aged British men might sound like they were making a joke of the incident if they used this form of language!
- 'fired at a student' – this sounds emotive, has connotations of intention rather than accident but, again, the meaning is ambiguous – did he actually hit the student or just aim in his direction?

b

Technique	Example
using emotive words	Charlie: 'ridiculous' Matt: 'bizarre … unbelievable'
exaggerating	Alan: 'stupidest thing … in twenty years of football' Charlie: 'I've never heard of anything as way out … as this'
putting added stress on a word (may be through intonation or use of intensifying adverbs as per examples)	Alan: **'stupidest'** Charlie: 'absolutely ridiculous' Matt: 'really unbelievable'
listing	Charlie: 'as (.) way out as whacky'
using repetition	Matt: 'it's bizarre (.) it's bizarre'

c Students should recognise the media's desire to shock and entertain as well as to inform. Emotive language choices often provoke strong responses, opinions and debate. By choosing to report in this way, news becomes a topic for discussion in society and the story can be perpetuated.

This task could be extended by asking students to listen to specific TV and radio news reports of current stories. They should identify examples of provocative language used and think about how this might shape the audience's response.

They could also script their own news reports for current events, using word choices to guide the audience into forming a certain opinion.

Check your learning

Students can test their knowledge of terminology by checking their definitions against the glossary at the back of the Student Book.

The task that follows encourages students to reflect on word choices and context. The answers below cover a range of suggestions; accept answers that are justified in a sensible way.

Context	Type of language and why?
Friends chatting	Colloquialisms/slang as it's a casual situation/they know each other well.
A speech from a political leader	Emotive language to inspire the audience. Jargon if addressing a specialist group.
Radio 1 music show	Colloquialisms/slang that would create a relaxed tone suitable for a younger audience. Emotive word choices if promoting a new artist or track.
Doctor's consultation room	Jargon, but nothing too specialist as it would also need to be explained. Colloquialisms to set the patient at ease.
Sports commentary	Emotive language to make the sport seem exciting.
Documentary on the natural world	Jargon connected to specialist subject, but again not too complex unless explained. Emotive language to create amazement at natural world.

4 Grammar and structure: Stories, text and tweets

AO focus

AO2:

- Understand variations in spoken language, explaining why language changes in relation to contexts.
- Evaluate the impact of spoken language choices in their own and others' use.

In this unit your students will:

- find out more about how spoken and written language differ
- learn about some of the structures of spoken language
- learn about how narratives can be put together in speech
- learn more about the features of computer-mediated communication and its forms and structures.

Key terms

Key terms the students are introduced to in this unit:

- Vague language
- Primary purpose
- Secondary purpose
- Statements (declaratives)
- Dynamic verbs
- Cohesion
- Conjunctions
- Signposting device
- Directive
- Imperative
- Modal verb
- Confirmation checks
- Ellipsis
- Quotative
- Discourse marker
- Computer-mediated communication (CMC)
- Compressed grammar
- Intonation
- Emoticon

Transcripts included in this unit

College gym instructor: introducing new students to gym equipment

Customer and sales assistant: conversation in a shop

Story dialogue extract: a girl on holiday

Mother and daughter: discussing a stolen phone

Zack's bike: a teenager's account

College principal: greeting new students

Radio interview: between a presenter and a video games expert

Protester's story: eyewitness account

Tweets and texts: computer-mediated-communication

Festival web forum: music fans discussing their favourite performers

See pp78–83 for photocopiable versions of these transcripts for students to work on.

Getting started

In this unit students find out more about the structures used in spoken language. This unit offers students the chance to see what a flexible and adaptable form spoken language can be. However, because speech is often spontaneous and often adapts to the situation, the ways in which we describe it need some new terms. Therefore, there is quite a lot of new terminology in this unit – more than in many others. Whether or not you want to use all of the terms is a decision you will make based on what you think your own students can cope with and what you think is most useful to your teaching.

Why use the terminology?

- It provides a quick way of identifying specific features.
- We use literary terms with poetry and drama, so why not for this kind of language analysis?
- It helps to establish spoken language as a form that is worthy of study.

The unit begins by looking at some of the structures that speech uses. A way into this is through thinking about how we vary things that we want to communicate depending on the form we're using.

Write down a set of ideas you'd like students to communicate to each other, such as arranging to meet a friend later that day, wishing someone luck

GCSE Spoken Language Skills
Section A: Spoken language skills

in a driving test, saying happy birthday to a cousin or asking someone if they've seen your house keys. Ask students to split into groups of four and role play these messages, using the following different forms of communication:

- text message
- phone call
- face-to-face talk
- letter.

Ask one member of each group to record the spoken forms and to keep the written ones. Use these as examples later in your work on the unit to draw attention to things like deixis, compressed grammar and vague language.

Structures in spoken and written language

Customer and sales assistant

This transcript looks at how spoken language often leaves gaps that we would not see in written language.

This is designed as a gentle starter activity to get students thinking about how we often shorten what we say compared to how it would be written in formal English. There are no entirely right or wrong answers for this activity, but the main patterns involve shortening the utterances in spoken form and removing words (often subject pronouns, like 'I', and verbs) because they are already clear from the context.

Activity 1

a The main difference is in the length of what is written or said. The written speech in the second extract uses full sentences while the real speech in the first extract is much more compressed.

b

Shortened version	Full version
'Two of the number 8 scratchcards please and a book of stamps'	'Please may I have two of the number 8 scratchcards and a book of stamps?'
'First or second class'	'Would you like first- or second-class stamps?'
'First please'	'I would like first-class stamps, please.'

c

Full version	Shortened version
'They're one pound fifty,' he replied.	'One pound fifty'
'Oh, how much are the small cones then?'	'What about the small cones'
'I've got one pound twenty-five'	'One pound twenty-five'

Vague language

Vague language is much more common in speech than in writing and can be used to soften what is said or make it sound less certain.

Activity 2

a This is designed to be a short pairs (or group) task, so you should prepare cards with the examples on to allow students to move them around and rank them on their tables. Students should rank the expressions as follows:

- At precisely 1.30pm
- At half past one, or near enough
- At one-ish
- At about lunchtime
- Later today, or something

b
- At half past one, or near enough: while a time is specified, it's still left a little open-ended.
- At one-ish: the addition of 'ish' signals a lack of concern over whether it's exactly that time.
- At about lunchtime: when is lunchtime for you? Some people might like to have their lunch at midday and others at 1.30pm. It's not a precise time.
- Later today, or something: this is the vaguest of all, because it only nods towards a later time of today and seems to signal a lack of concern through the 'or something'.

c

Certain	Vague
18,997 people went to the game.	About 20,000 people went to the game.
I will see you at 8.45pm, exactly 24 hours from now.	I'll see you tomorrow night at quarter to nine.
A group of 6 men caused £15,550 damage to the bus.	Half a dozen men caused thousands of pounds' worth of damage to the bus.
I'd like three 1 litre bottles of the sugar-free cola drink flavoured with vegetable extract.	I'd like three large bottles of diet Coke/diet Pepsi, please.
Can you get me a sandwich, baguette, roll or wrap, please?	Can you get me a sandwich or something like that, please?

Unit 4 Grammar and structure:
Stories, text and tweets

Review and reflect

a Vague language can help signal something about our personalities. We might come across as easy-going, carefree or relaxed. Alternatively, others might see it as too laid-back, perhaps lacking care over specifics. It depends a lot on perceptions.

b Some of the reasons why people may choose to use precise language are as follows:
- because precision is required (exact directions, technical terms, matters of life and death)
- because someone wants to make a point
- because someone feels strongly about their view
- to be as truthful and accurate as possible.

c Some of the reasons why people may choose to use vague language are as follows:
- to appear less assertive and more cooperative
- to soften harsh or unpleasant news
- to avoid disagreement
- to appear less bothered about something
- to signal an easy-going attitude
- to avoid appearing too precise.

Zack's bike

Quotatives are common structures in speech and are useful to look at because they differ so much between age groups and even areas. There may even be other quotatives that you are aware of from your usage or knowledge and that students might have come across (like 'I was all', which hasn't been included in the original list).

Activity 3

a 'I was like', 'he goes', 'I was like', 'he was like', 'I was like', 'he goes', 'I was like'.

Student answers will vary depending on their chosen quotatives.

b The second activity depends very much on the students themselves to identify which ones they use, but if they are not forthcoming with this, move straight on to the third task in this activity.

c This activity sets up a mini-research task for students. Encouraging them to think about how they would find their own data is the aim here and, if they actually go ahead and get some data, then this could be helpful for assessment further down the line.

Telling stories

This subsection deals with the structures and devices used in spoken storytelling. The narrative structure model used later is a simplified version of the American linguist William Labov's approach, and is intended to avoid overloading students with too much extra terminology yet offers the same basic structure that Labov uses.

College principal

This transcript demonstrates the use of signposting, which is an effective way of signalling to listeners what you will be speaking about in detail later on or that you are moving on from one idea to another.

Activity 1

a The signposting techniques used in the opening transcript (college gym instructor) include: 'before we start', 'then' and 'The first thing I need to stress'.

b The signposting devices used by the speaker range from the short ('Hello and welcome', 'this morning', 'but first') to the more developed ('I will be introducing you to …').

c The reasons for signposting are to offer a brief overview of what she is about to go on to talk about and to prepare students for what they are about to hear.

Radio interview

This transcript makes use of discourse markers – words or expressions that draw listeners' attention to what is coming next.

Activity 2

a Four discourse markers: 'So', 'Well', 'In fact', 'however'.

b 'So' and 'well' seem to signal something new about to be said. 'In fact' and 'however' rely on something being said before, in the first case to emphasise a possibly intriguing fact, and with the latter a contrast.

c i Most of them are used to link ideas together ('so' being a clear example) and signal where the talk is going.

   ii 'Alright guys' and 'OK guys' are used to do both.

Protester's story

This transcript features a narrative following the simple structure of scene setting, event and reaction.

Activity 3

a

Scene setting	Basically err (.) I was at Tower Hill tube with Paul (.) err waiting for Gary and Rashid to get there (.) there was like hundreds of people (.) all with placards and banners (.) people were meeting up with their mates (1)
Event	I could hear police horses coming closer and then this guy near me shouted they're charging they're charging and it was like **woah** (.) looked round and there was four or five mounted police bombing towards us (.) we just dived out of the way into this newsagents' doorway and they just like swept by (1)
Reaction	don't think I've ever come that close to getting trampled before

b In the first two parts (scene setting and event) most events are conveyed in the past tense (sometimes the past progressive, e.g. 'people were meeting up'), although some direct speech is in the present tense (e.g. 'this guy near me shouted they're charging they're charging'). In the final part (reaction), it is in the present tense ('don't think' and 'I've ever come'). This is typical of storytelling where events are recounted but reactions are more immediate.

c The more dramatic words used might be the creation of scale by using 'hundreds of people' (perhaps linking back to vague language earlier), 'charging', 'woah', 'bombing', 'dived', 'swept' and 'trampled'. All of these are verbs, apart from the interjection 'woah'.

Plenary activity

Depending on how securely your classes have dealt with the ideas in this unit, you might want to draw some of these different strands together with a plenary task. For example, ask them to prepare a poster or fact sheet that introduces next year's new students to the features of spoken and written storytelling.

Stretch yourself

Suggest that students go out and record friends or family members and then look at how their stories are told. Make sure they are aware of the ethics of recording others and that they seek their permission. Another good source of material is the BBC Listening Project, http://www.bbc.co.uk/radio4/features/the-listening-project, which features a broad range of conversations between friends and family members on themes such as education, family, sport and war, all of which could be used by you or your students.

Multimodal texts

While texts, tweets and emails aren't strictly spoken language, they are treated as such (or at least as *blended forms*) by many of the GCSE specifications.

One way to start this part of the unit is to prepare some emoticon cards – smiley face, winking face, sad face, face-palm, confused face – to use in a starter activity. Prepare a few sample sentences such as those below and then ask students to rewrite the sentence to reflect the mood or tone of the emoticon card you hold up. So, for example, they would need to think of how to change the language of 'You are looking really good today' to something more appropriate when you show the sad face emoticon card.

- I hope you are feeling well.
- You are looking really good today.
- I miss you.
- What did you say about me to your friend?

By doing this, students will be able to see how much work body language has to do in a normal face-to-face conversation and how much emoticons can convey. It might also lead to some discussions about different interpretations we draw from the same messages and how we all have different ways of reading the same thing.

Tweets and texts

These extracts are all forms of computer-mediated communication (CMC). As well as using compressed grammar, users of CMC tend to abbreviate more regularly than in formal writing.

Activity 1

a Abbreviations:

RT = retweet

LUFC = Leeds United Football Club

4 = for

Compressed grammar:

(I) so want to believe this

(It has been) on, nearly complete, off

b Extra punctuation:

!!!!!

???

!!

c Ask students to discuss what these might mean in their different contexts. Why have they been used and what do they add? Some of these meanings might be disbelief, surprise, shocked outrage or confusion.

Unit 4 Grammar and structure: Stories, text and tweets

Text messages

These text messages show examples of compressed grammar and abbreviated words.

Activity 2

a Most compressed listed first:

I'm so sorry, i no it mite jus b wrds but im really sori 4 2day

Leanne babe quik question do u think frm wen u last saw me i have put on weight? Txt bk asap xax

Hey you ok? Heard you weren't feelin well ...

If I don't remember to call you, flash me after 4.30pm. Carla.

b

Compressed version	Standard English version
Hey you ok? Heard you weren't feelin well ...	Hey are you OK? I heard that you were not feeling well.
I'm so sorry, i no it mite jus b wrds but im really sori 4 2day	I'm so sorry. I know that it might just be words, but I'm really sorry for what happened today.
If I don't remember to call you, flash me after 4.30pm. Carla.	If I don't remember to call you, give me a ring after 4.30pm. Carla.
Leanne babe quik question do u think frm wen u last saw me i have put on weight? Txt bk asap xax	Leanne, babe, I've got a quick question for you: do you think that from when you last saw me that I have put on weight? Text me back as soon as possible.

c This will depend largely on what your own students come up with, but recent research suggests that use of smartphones and predictive text are leading to fewer 'textisms' than before. Also, many teenagers now claim that abbreviations are for younger kids. It would be interesting to see if they say this but still use abbreviations themselves.

Stretch yourself

Once again, this kind of task is a good way of drawing strands from this unit together. Divide the class into groups and assign each group a different form of CMC to explore. One group looks at the language used in texts, another group looks at the language of Xbox Live gaming, another at MSN and another at Twitter. Each group gathers examples of communication from these forms and presents them back to the class, drawing out the potential, key features and possible limitations of each form.

Festival web forum

Students look at another form of multimodal text by examining the web forum posts. Here we have a slightly longer exchange, which starts to offer a bit more interaction between the participants. Encourage more able students to look at how different individual styles (idiolects) of each poster might be noted by grouping together all of the posts from each person and looking for patterns.

Activity 3

a i Examples of ellipsis:

Poster 2: (the) best band for me was foo fighters – (they were) amaaaaazing

Poster 3: (I) thought they were rubbish. (They were) Boring and played to long and (they) should of done teen spirit

Poster 1: (I) can't agree with that!!

Poster 2: (I) cant believe my eyes

ii Examples of abbreviations: 'bout', 'n', 'nuff'.

iii Example of emoticon: :-O

iv Example of extra punctuation: '!!'

v Examples of non-standard language:
- Spelling used to reflect sound of voice: stretching out the aaaaa of amazing.
- To and of in poster 3's first contribution are both spelt incorrectly (to = too) and (should of = should have/should've).
- Poster 2 misses out an apostrophe in cant.

b Different posters use different forms of the same word or expression. For example, posters 1 and 2 write can't/cant differently. Poster 4 capitalises the proper name The Cure, while few others capitalise at all.

c We each have our own individual spoken and written styles, so there's also every reason to have our own multimodal styles.

Check your learning

There is enough material in this unit alone to get students started on their own work on spoken and multimodal language for the controlled assessment.

The two Stretch yourself tasks (on pages 53 and 56) could be used as the start of data gathering for groups of students. You could then set variations on previous controlled assessment questions to steer them towards written work on these questions.

5 Planned and unplanned speech: The right words at the right time

AO focus

AO2:

- Understand variations in spoken language, explaining why language changes in relation to contexts.
- Evaluate the impact of spoken language choices in their own and others' use.

In this unit your students will:

- study planned, unplanned and semi-planned speech
- consider different types of talk
- learn about structures and features of different types of speech
- analyse how writers use spoken language on screen and in books
- look at multimodal forms of communication.

Key terms

Key terms the students are introduced to in this unit:

- Scheme
- Rhetoric
- Ad-lib
- Oratory
- Context-dependent
- Turn-taking

Transcripts included in this unit

Michelle Obama speech: to the Democratic Party convention, September 2012

Bill Clinton script: given to journalists before he delivered his speech

Bill Clinton actual speech: delivered in September 2012

Xbox video game: boys playing the same game, on the same team but in different countries

Tour of Britain cycle race: live commentary

Football: text commentary

Classroom talk: teacher introducing guests to the class

Remote control family talk: a transcript

Pigeon English: an extract from the novel

Friday Night Dinner: a transcript from the TV show

See pp84–92 for photocopiable versions of these transcripts for students to work on.

Getting started

In this unit, students look at different forms of speech and some computer-mediated communication (CMC). By the end of this unit they will have been introduced to:

- planned political speeches and how they are delivered to appear more spontaneous
- unplanned, spontaneous talk, and how writers use represented speech in their work.

Speaking and listening

The introductory activity in the unit offers a good starter for all students of whatever ability. One of the key skills for students to develop in their work on spoken language is the ability to reflect on the language that they use and hear around them.

a Encourage students to think about the different types of talk they hear on a typical day and how it can be classified. You could consider turning this starter into a longer activity by asking students to keep a log over a week, rather than a day, and then recording snippets of different talk that they hear, presenting extracts back to the class.

b Colloquial/casual talk among friends; prepared and planned talk at an assembly or start of a lesson; structured conversation in class between teachers and students; talk on the phone; talk on the college radio; persuasive talk at an assembly ... all of these are possibilities and there are probably many more.

Stretch yourself

Building up a bank of spoken audio extracts is a good way of bolstering your own resources for use with other classes. Political speeches can be found on YouTube or via links on the websites of broadsheet newspapers in the UK and US. Students can be encouraged to transcribe the speech they have recorded and get to grips with the difficulties and demands of spoken language study at an early stage.

Unit 5 Planned and unplanned speech:
The right words at the right time

Prepared speeches

Students will probably be quite familiar with prepared speeches from their work in KS3, but this section starts to focus a bit more on the spoken language frameworks that can be applied to such speeches.

The annotated transcript flags up many of the key features of planning that are shown in a speech like this and the first activity asks students to think about other types of planned speech that they come across in their lives. For example, at work there might be a planned talk given to employees with latest sales targets, or inspection criteria. At a conference, there may be a planned introduction to a planned lecture. At an awards night, there may be a planned speech praising a prize-winner, followed by a planned acceptance speech.

Bill Clinton script/actual speech

Good speakers will often use a script for the basis of what they say. The first extract is a script of Bill Clinton's speech, whilst the second extract is a transcript of the actual speech.

Activity 2

a The differences between the two extracts can be seen in the table below.

b

c Much of what Clinton adds here takes the form of more colloquial language that strikes up a more friendly relationship with his audience. He addresses them directly in the spoken version, engages in more of a conversation with them and even adds some quite folksy stylings – expressions such as 'I'm fixing to …' which reflect his southern US roots. His use of rhetorical question and response in the penultimate line of the table above also helps to make this sound less crafted and more engaging.

Planned or unplanned talk

Many other types of talk are planned, although they may contain elements that are unplanned.

Activity 3

There are different ways of interpreting the levels of planning/spontaneity in some of these examples, so some comments are included for each:

- A sermon by a priest in a church: sermons are often written beforehand, so will be quite planned (ranked at the top of the diamond). However, some spontaneous elements might be included to achieve a more immediate effect, and this can depend very much on the type of church and the nature of the priest.

Words and phrases added in actual speech	Words and phrases changed in actual speech
Now, look	'I understand the challenge we face' changed to 'Here's the challenge he faces and the challenge all of you who support him face'.
I get it. I know it. I've been there.	'I experienced the same thing in 1994 and early 1995' changed to 'I had the same thing happen in 1994 and early '95'.
If you look at the numbers	'No President – not me or any of my predecessors could have repaired all the damage in just four years' changed to 'No president – no president, not me, not any of my predecessors, no one could have fully repaired all the damage that he found in just four years'.
The difference this time is purely in the circumstances	'I believe that with all my heart' changed to 'With all my heart, I believe it'.
Listen to me, now	
You will feel it.	
Folks, whether the American people believe what I just said or not may be the whole election. I just want you to know that I believe it.	
Now, why do I believe it? I'm fixing to tell you why.	
a shared sense of community	

- Answering a phone call from a friend: knowing who you are talking to can lead to a much more spontaneous exchange, so this would probably come lower on the ranking.
- Answering a phone call from a number you do not recognise: it's more likely that you would have a traditional opening sequence to a call from an unknown number, so this might not necessarily be planned, but would fit into a 'scheme' of what is expected.
- A teacher starting a lesson that's being observed by an Ofsted inspector: the lesson would have been planned in advance and the key activities would have been worked out and timed, in all probability. However, the exchanges between teacher and students would also have a degree of spontaneity because neither of the speakers would know exactly what the other is going to say.
- A street charity collector trying to get you to sign up to their cause: most charity collectors have a pre-prepared patter, often practising using a script, but they also respond to the audience's reactions and vary what they are saying depending on answers they are given. This would probably appear nearer the top end of the diamond.
- Three friends playing Xbox live together over the internet: this would be the most spontaneous of all, because there would be no knowing what was going to happen and the fact that the players are communicating online means that there would be less ability to judge what someone else might be about to say.
- A parent asking you about your day at school: this would be fairly spontaneous, but it is a fairly common scenario so might follow a scheme.
- Buying a book of stamps from a shop assistant: there is room for spontaneity here, but it follows an expected scheme, so probably not planned as such, but nearer the top end of the diamond rather than the bottom.
- A radio presenter commentating on a Paralympics event: the commentator would be responding to events as they happened, so this would be highly spontaneous, but the event itself may be something they have commentated on many times before and therefore it might be seen as following an expected pattern. Much closer to the bottom end of the diamond rather than the top.

Stretch yourself

This activity picks up on the strands elsewhere in this unit and gets students to set up their own experiment. This is the sort of data that can then be used in preparation for controlled assessment, or just be used in class to focus attention on key differences between planned and unplanned talk.

Spontaneous and semi-planned speech

Xbox Live video game

Unplanned speech is one of the most common types of speech that we use. Spontaneous speech is well suited to dealing with how things change in a conversation and being flexible.

Activity 1

L: over there (1) yeah (.) wait (.) wait

F: where are they

L: can't see them yet (.) just //

F: //there look he's coming over (.) he's crossing the bridge=

L: =get him (.) Get him quick (.)

F: I need more ammo

L: you've just got to hit him

F: got to get to cover

L: wait (.) cover me (.) he's in the barn (.) you come to me (.) yeah

F: right (.) can't see him (.) where are you

L: by the wall (.) next (.) next to the oil drums (.) You get here and we'll (1) stop (.) wait (.) he's there in the (.) the window

F: who got him

L: what

F: someone got him

L: not me

F: uh-oh

a The highlighted examples above illustrate some key features: responses to players' actions (in the form of 'yeah'); repetition to reinforce directions from one player to another ('wait (.) wait'); use of present progressive to describe action as it is happening ('coming over (.) he's crossing the bridge'); and responses to actions in the game ('uh-oh').

b The speech is spontaneous because so much of it is clearly unplanned and responding to the gameplay. It's probably spontaneous, too, because the players are not thinking that much about what they are saying; they are thinking much more about the action of the game itself. The game players are likely to be well known to each other, so language is not being used to impress, but to carry out quite functional tasks.

c It's unlikely that there would be that many differences. Even though the players are at a distance, their attention is still on the same thing.

Tour of Britain cycle race

This transcript demonstrates another form of spontaneous speech – live commentary.

Activity 2

a The following examples indicate that the commentators are describing something as it happens:

'oh there's a crash'

'ooh'

'look at that'

'(.) and Borgini='

b This activity highlights some of the key features of live commentaries, including the use of the present tense (e.g. 'The flags are out'), progressive aspect ('just rolling away'), ellipsis ('Borgini from Liquigas (is) down') and deixis ('and Brett Lancaster there').

c The commentators take on different roles, often with C2 acting as the expert cyclist, offering more detail to the running commentary given by C1. C2 often shows agreement with C1 (latching on with 'yeah') before adding more detail from a cyclist's perspective.

Stretch yourself

The text commentary is a good example of how closely CMC forms of language can mimic the spoken forms they are based on, while offering text and images on the screen to read.

The more able student should be able to see the way in which ellipsis is used in a way very similar to spoken language. They might also note the ways in which different 'speakers' take 'turns', as in the cycling commentary.

Most students should be able to see that the commentary gives the appearance of being spontaneous and running alongside the action, but will be aware that the text could have been edited for accuracy and to restructure ideas.

All students should be able to see that, while the text is unplanned, it follows the same expectations of a spoken commentary.

Classroom talk

If the political speech sits at one end of the prepared continuum, and the commentaries at the other, then the classroom talk transcript probably sits somewhere in the middle. While the situation is very familiar and the turn-taking quite formulaic, the actual content of each turn is not necessarily planned. Linguists, Sinclair and Coulthard (1975) came up with the IRF (Initiation–Response–Feedback) structure of classroom discourse, and without going into too much detail, this basic idea can be applied to what happens in the classroom talk extract here.

Activity 3

a The teacher's utterances sound more planned than the students' and this might be indicated by things like the length and grammatical complexity of what he says (for example, the clause embedding in his first turn) in comparison to the relatively short turns of most of the students.

b The teacher keeps the students responding by using a number of questions, some aimed at specific students, others more open to the whole class. He also refers back to the work the students have done before and keeps them involved by explaining how what they have done relates to what they are going to move on to do. On a couple of occasions, he uses discourse markers ('Right', 'OK' and the quite forceful 'Now listen') to draw attention to important points he wishes to make.

c The teacher uses the IRF pattern in the following exchange:

A: right what did you make a speech about

D: cannabis

A: cannabis (.) and what did you say about cannabis

The teacher asks questions and gets responses, which he then builds on with further questions. Looking at turn-taking in 'asymmetrical' exchanges like these is useful for grasping the dynamics of other conversations in which power and status are perhaps less evenly distributed.

Represented speech

These are fairly straightforward activities that draw students' attention to the ways in which

GCSE Spoken Language Skills
Section A: Spoken language skills

writers often use some of the characteristics of real speech in their dialogue, but not all of them.

Remote-control family talk

This transcript is fairly typical of many conversations that go on in families where multiple topics are being dealt with at the same time and people are often referring back to previous conversations.

Activity 1

a It might be difficult to follow because speaker A asks a question and speaker B replies with what seems to be an irrelevant response, while speaker D's comment is met with a response from speaker C that takes the topic away from the initial one being put forward – the whereabouts of the remote control. Also, the use of deixis (demonstrative pronouns like 'that' and 'there', for example) means that you would have to know where they were pointing or what they were looking at. You could link in some of the work from Unit 6 here too.

b Students might want to remove the first turn from speaker A and then keep the topics in the order as they appear after that.

c Quite a lot of the language here depends on context, so if you were scripting this you might want to make it clearer which things in the environment are being referred to. Also, you might want to add some more content to each turn to make it a bit less reliant on knowing what has gone before.

Pigeon English

This extract is an example of written speech that is designed to look or sound like speech.

Activity 2

a The extract from *Pigeon English* makes use of several features of spontaneous speech, including some slang ('well skilful' and 'the pen', i.e. the penitentiary/prison) and quite rapid turn-taking.

b The effect of this is less precise to gauge, but this kind of naturalistic dialogue often creates a sense of quick-fire talk and a flavour of age, region and ethnicity that might not be conveyed by written Standard English.

c The author has used other features of speech, including context-dependent language (references with pronouns back to things that have already been talked about or that refer to objects around the speakers), a tag question ('innit'), and a confirmation check that's similar to a tag question in its function ('OK?').

Friday Night Dinner

This is an extract of dialogue from a TV comedy.

Activity 3

a As above, there are several noticeable features of spoken language used here, such as the turn-taking and references to immediate environment (pointing at objects and places). There are also some uses of very short, elliptical utterances (as in the last three turns).

b One thing that is clear is the lack of simultaneous speech (except for the one instance towards the end between D and M). There also appears to be some deliberate shaping and repetition of language for emphasis; A echoes M when referring to the broken toilet, and the echoing of 'crap' at the end is for humorous emphasis.

c When writing for a listening/viewing audience, some aspects of genuine speech can cause confusion – overlaps and interruptions, inaudible speech, turns that don't follow the normal rules of adjacent pairs – so turns are more likely to be latched than overlapping.

Stretch yourself

One way to ensure that students can see the differences between real and scripted talk is to get them to transform one form into another. Using transcripts from this unit and others in the Student Book (perhaps taking the annotated transcripts at the start of each unit to begin with), ask students to work in groups to turn genuine talk into any of the following different forms:

- dramatic monologues
- soap opera scripts
- dialogue from a novel
- drama scripts

Check your learning

	A	B	C	D	E	F	G	H	I	J
Spontaneous speech			X	X	X			X		X
Rhetorical technique	X	X							X	
Ad-lib		X	X	X	X		X		X	X
Colloquial				X	X	X		X		X
Scheme	X	X			X	X	X		X	
Context-dependent speech			X	X	X	X		X	X	X

A A political speech
B A sermon by a priest
C A chat between friends
D An apology you have to make when you have been caught doing something you should not have been
E A conversation with a shop assistant when you are buying something
F A weather forecast on the TV
G A newsreader's introduction to a programme
H An online chat with a group of friends
I A speech at a school council meeting
J A TV chef explaining a recipe

Some possibilities are suggested in the table above. There are some areas for debate, notably over ad-libs and schemes, but check definitions of these and make sure students are clear when they are likely to occur:

- Ad-libs tend to be moments of spontaneity in otherwise planned talk.
- Schemes are formulaic structures that often appear in exchanges we have on a regular basis.

6 Implied meanings: Why don't you say what you mean?

AO focus

AO2:

- Understand variations in spoken language, explaining why language changes in relation to contexts.
- Evaluate the impact of spoken language choices in their own and others' use.

In this unit your students will:

- learn to how to differentiate between implied and explicit meanings
- explore how politeness takes different forms according to the context of the conversation.

Key terms

Key terms the students are introduced to in this unit:

- Explicit meaning
- Direct
- Subtext
- Command

Transcripts included in this unit

The Inbetweeners: an annotated TV comedy script

Educating Essex: a reality TV script

Channel 4 news: the presenter and politician Chloë Smith discuss the Government's U-turn on fuel tax

The Family: a reality TV programme showing a mother and her son discussing school

Death of a Salesman: three excerpts

See pp93–98 for photocopiable versions of these transcripts for students to work on.

Getting started

In this unit students study the concept of subtext and are asked to consider not just how we use language but why. The activities are designed to help students recognise when people imply meanings and to consider how the context of a conversation affects these decisions. *The Inbetweeners* transcript immediately shows how context affects how we talk to each other.

The Inbetweeners

Speaking and listening

This activity is a way of getting students to use language carefully and to adapt to a role.

It would be useful to give the person playing the role of the student a list of reasons why he should not attend the assemblies so that they can sustain the conversation. Look for students' ability to stay in role throughout and to adapt their language to the role that they are playing. At the top level, some students will be able to use language persuasively to get their own way. For example, a head teacher who makes statements such as, 'You mustn't be afraid to meet new people, you know', or a new student who makes statements such as, 'I like to get to know my new friends in a less-intimidating environment'.

'That is not what I meant': implied meanings and misunderstandings

The first activities allow all students to access the idea of implied meaning by using short snippets of conversations.

Speaking and listening

Students should easily see that there are opportunities to misunderstand simple utterances that we use every day. The activity is an ideal starter as it encourages discussion of the topic by using a situation that most can relate to.

a   The child answered the question as if the adult had just wanted to know his mother's whereabouts rather than wanting to talk to her.

The child believes that the question 'Don't you think you've had enough?' is asking his opinion rather than denying the request.

b   The conversations would be clearer if the following phrases were used:

Adult: hi. Let me speak to your mummy

Or:

Mum: you are not allowed any more Coke because you have already had enough.

c i   Although the implied meaning is that it is dinner time, the child may just answer yes or no based on how they feel.

   ii The child will not recognise that the parent is indicating that they want to finish playing.

Unit 6 Implied meanings:
Why don't you say what you mean?

iii The child may not realise that the parent is cross or wants the child to tidy up.

iv The child may not recognise that the parent thinks that they have been playing for too long.

v The child may not realise that the parent is telling them off for running away.

Identifying implied meanings

Activity 1

a and b Both of these activities require students to analyse how meaning is implied by one-word answers and how they can be interpreted in a number ways. The important part is getting students to justify their answers.

c Looking at the alternative meanings of words and phrases as shown in the table below helps students to understand the concept of implied meanings. The completed table is just a suggested model.

A phrase which could have more than one meaning	One meaning	An alternative meaning
'I'm starving'	'Let's stop for food'	'Give me some of your food'
'It's cold in here'	'I'm cold, do you agree?'	'Shut the door, it's letting the draught in'
'Don't look at me like that'	'Stop looking at me, you're making me feel awkward'	'I don't like the look on your face. Change it.'
'Something smells tasty'	'You are a good cook and your food smells nice'	'I would like some of what you are cooking'

'Don't talk to me like that': politeness and context

The concept of politeness is key for students to understand why we choose to be indirect in some contexts and more direct in others.

'Give me the phone'

The list of utterances all have the same request, 'can I use the phone after you?' However, some are more polite than others.

Ask students to question whether they use similar language to that used in the examples and what effect it may have on their success in getting their own way. This activity works best if the utterances are cut out and pairs or groups of three decide on an order. The discussion that students have about where to place the examples is as important as where they are placed. In discussion, guide the groups to explain in which context the requests would be acceptable.

Speaking and listening

Ask students to complete the table to reinforce the idea that we use different types of politeness depending on who we are talking to. Students should come to the conclusion that implied meanings are usually a more polite way of using language and are often used in formal situations. Again, the completed table suggests some answers that students may come up with.

To your grandma	*Granny, do you have a pen I can use?*
To a teacher	Please could I borrow a pen?
To your mum	Can I use that?
To a shopkeeper	Would I be able to borrow a pen?
To a friend	Give us your pen a minute.
To your sister/brother	Where's that pen gone?
To a stranger	Excuse me, you wouldn't have a pen that I could borrow, would you?

Educating Essex

This transcript has been annotated to give students an idea of how they can pinpoint specific words and phrases to show how the role of pupil and teacher are framed according to their expectations.

Students should pick up on how the conversation has a subtext of humour and that, despite being limited by role in what they can say to each other, both Mr Drew and Charlotte appear to enjoy the conversation. The activities then move away from the transcript and try to get students to think of contexts where implied meaning is more usual.

Activity 1

a The word 'amuse' has been used by Mr Drew because he is implying that Charlotte's laughter is rude.

b i Charlotte can't answer directly because Mr Drew is her teacher and she must avoid being directly rude to him. Students may point out that her refusal to give in to Mr Drew may indicate a rebellious streak or a quite comfortable relationship with Mr Drew.

ii 'Oh my God' implies that Charlotte can't believe that Mr Drew won't stop asking her if he's amused and that she thinks that the conversation has become ridiculous.

GCSE Spoken Language Skills
Section A: Spoken language skills

c There are a wide range of contexts that could be discussed, but students will probably identify many transactional situations such as shops, hairdressers, with friends' parents, with distant relations.

Channel 4 News

This news interview is a good example of implied meanings and students generally understand the way in which the politician has to avoid the truth while the presenter can be more explicit and direct.

There are other political interviews that you could watch with students to discuss the way in which politicians tend to give euphemistic, jargon-heavy answers compared with the interviewer's direct and usually impartial questions.

Activity 2

a Students should identify the fact that Krishnan is implying that the Government does not have the money for a tax cut.

b Students should also see that Chloë Smith's aim is to show that the tax cut for fuel is a bonus; some good and unexpected news.

c Students should identify that Krishnan tends to interrupt when the interviewee tries to change the topic or use jargon-heavy answers.

Stretch yourself

This task is challenging. It would be useful to either give students information about a current event or to ask them to research a news story that interests them. They will need to have a clear idea of the facts and issues that are part of the interview. This activity also works in groups of three, where two students role play the interview and one student observes the use of language, noting down interruptions and implied meanings.

The activity asks students to role play a *Newsnight*-type interview and to follow a structure similar to the Channel 4 news transcript just studied. Look for the way in which the student role playing the interviewer uses techniques similar to Krishnan's, such as direct questions, repetition of a key point and interruptions. The student role playing the politician has a more difficult task because they will need to use jargon and longer utterances to try to avoid a direct answer.

Plenary activity

As part of a plenary activity, students could plot on a continuum the contexts that are the most direct moving down to those that are the least direct, ensuring that the link between formality, context and implied meaning is clearly understood.

Using implied meaning to persuade

As a starter to this section you could ask students to write down a list of times when they have had to persuade people. With whole-class feedback, ask students to explain how they persuade and whether their language differs according to their audience. Typical responses could be:

- persuading a parent to give them a lift
- persuading a sibling or friend to lend them something
- asking a teacher for a homework extension.

The Family

After the starter discussion, students should be ready to look at *The Family* transcript which is about a boy, Tom, persuading his mum to take him out of the school that he hates. The activities focus on close reading questions and the aim is to encourage students to find specific words that will allow them to analyse Tom's use of persuasion.

Activity 1

a i Students will probably identify emotive words like 'push', 'too hard', 'hate', 'shout' and 'strict' and then link them to Tom's purpose.

ii and iii The evaluation of Tom's success requires students to look at the mum's words and hopefully they will notice that her tone becomes more assertive and less understanding towards the end of the conversation, suggesting that Tom's strategies haven't really worked.

b i and ii When looking at the words that Mum uses, students should be able to recognise that her strategy mixes praise with authority and that this strategy is effective in this conversation. The model paragraph is designed to encourage students to move away from describing and discussing implied meaning and to practise writing analytically using detailed examples from the transcript.

c Students should be able to use specific words and phrases that they have picked out in earlier activities and organise these individual features into an analysis of the whole conversation. Therefore, by identifying Tom's attempts to use persuasive language in a and his mum's response in b, students have evidence to analyse the effectiveness of implied meanings in the transcript as a whole.

Unit 6 Implied meanings:
Why don't you say what you mean?

Activity 2

This offers your students the chance to analyse what Mum wants to achieve in the conversation. Get your students to use the short extract as a prompt for their answers.

Speaking and listening

These activities are quite challenging because they ask students to incorporate some of the examples of implied meaning covered earlier in the unit. In order to prepare for the scenarios, it may be useful to discuss each context as a whole class. Most students will have some experience of the scenarios, so sharing their knowledge will help to make the contexts clear.

Pairs should be given time to discuss the scenarios and plan what sort of direction the conversation will go in. In order to focus students on the concept of implied meanings, you could write some starting sentences on the board to scaffold their response. Examples could be:

Scenario 1:

I thought that this shop …

Other shops would …

It looks a bit …

You do know that worn items …

Scenario 2:

I've sold nothing …

Do you like cooking …

I've got to …

I haven't got …

Scenario 3:

Look at that one …

Don't get me wrong, I'm …

I didn't see …

Well, not all …

In order to assess speaking and listening, pairs could peer assess, with a brief criteria from your exam board. Pairs could listen to each other's role play and give feedback on:

- how well the role was sustained
- their use of implied meaning
- their ability to keep the conversation fluent.

Plenary activity

As part of a plenary activity, you could discuss how successful the different role plays were in illustrating the use of implied meaning. Was there any scenario where it was particularly difficult to avoid being direct?

Arguments and quarrels

This final section is designed to encourage students to look at subtext and to explore how writers use implied meanings to suggest ideas to their audience.

The activities all lead to character analysis through the examination of implied meanings, so a good starter might be to look at character types.

Death of a Salesman (1)

Working with the transcripts, students can see how they can interpret meanings and relationships without the playwright being explicit. Implied meanings are used to create tension and to reveal character.

Activity 1

a Students may identify most of the adjectives to describe the brothers' relationship, and this could lead into a discussion that Happy is quite cautious of Biff, but that he is not necessarily uncaring or hostile.

b The table should be quite straightforward now that students are familiar with the idea of implied meaning. Possible answers are as follows:

Line from the play	What it really means
Example: 'He's not mocking you, he –'	He's not mocking you he is just disappointed in you.
'He just wants you to make good'	You've been drifting and it upsets him.
'Something's happening to him'	I think he's going mad.
'That you're still kind of up in the air'	You don't have any stability in your life.
'There's one or two other things depressing him, Happy'	I know things that you don't know about.
'Just don't lay it all to me.'	There are other reasons for his behaviour.
'But I think if you got started'	Why don't you just get a job like most people?

c By identifying the non-fluency features, students can apply some of the terminology that they learned in Unit 1. They should pick up on features such as pauses, the use of hedging ('kind of') and fillers such as 'I mean' and Happy's unfinished utterances. They should be able to suggest that the non-fluency features add to the audience's understanding that Happy is uncertain in the conversation.

Death of a Salesman (2)

In the next transcript, the conversation between Biff, Linda and Happy shows students

GCSE Spoken Language Skills
Section A: Spoken language skills

that a seemingly ordinary conversation can be full of implied meaning and subtext. The differentiation between topic and purpose has been explored in Unit 2.

Activity 2

a Students should be able to suggest that, although the conversation's topic is about getting old, the purpose is to discuss the changes in their family dynamic.

b Students may suggest that when Biff says 'I don't want my old pal looking old', he feels that things have changed since he's been gone.

c Students may discuss the idea that Biff seems to like his mum more than his dad and they recognise that this isn't stated, just 'implied'.

Death of a Salesman (3)

The last set of activities in this section focuses on the scene between Willy and his boss Howard. The intention is that students will clearly understand Howard's implied meanings and notice that Willy does not and that his refusal to understand Howard's language shows that he is in denial.

Activity 3

a Students should identify lines such as 'you can't go to Boston for us', 'I don't want you to represent us', 'I think you need a good long rest', 'why don't your sons give you a hand?', 'tell them that you're tired'. Students may be quite frustrated with Willy by the end of the conversation.

b This frustration should help students to complete the table about Willy's reasons for refusing to understand Howard. The comments only refer to the short excerpt used, and so shouldn't make any reference to other parts of the play.

Speaking and listening

This activity works well after watching an episode of the TV show *The Apprentice*, when one of the contestants is fired. Students could discuss the way in which applicants for the job try to persuade Lord Sugar to employ them.

Plenary activity

Get students to carry out some investigations into implied meanings. They could record and transcribe a short section of a family argument from a TV programme. A soap opera such as *EastEnders* or *Coronation Street* could provide good source material. Get them to look for patterns where:

- people avoid saying what they really mean
- people use non-fluency features when they are unsure of how their comments will be taken
- they use questions rather than statements or commands.

See if they can identify implied meanings and the reasons that they may be used.

Check your learning

Ask students to reflect on some of the different types of implied meanings, as well as trying to identify, with a specific example, how we can recognise when people are being indirect.

Students should come up with four different types of situation:

- misunderstandings
- to be polite or kind
- the role that we are expected to play within a context
- to persuade and get our own way.

Statement	Agree/disagree	Explanation and evidence
Willy is desperate to keep his job.	Agree	I agree because Willy wilfully misunderstands Howard's attempt to sack him.
Willy does not think his sons can help him financially.	Disagree	He is afraid that they won't want to, but he is ashamed of asking them for help. For him, it shows weakness: 'I'm not a cripple!'
Howard is kind to Willy.	Somewhat agree	Howard tries to soften the blow of getting the sack by being vague and saying things like, 'you need a good long rest'. However, he becomes quite frustrated towards the end and loses patience. His last line is abrupt and cruel: 'pull yourself together'.
Willy is bad at his job.	Agree	Howard sees Willy as a liability and says, 'I don't want you to represent us'.
Howard patronises Willy.	Agree	I agree because Howard calls Willy 'kid' even though Willy is close to retirement age.
Willy is optimistic about the future.	Disagree	He is desperate to work and can only see one way forward, by carrying on working for Howard.

There are plenty of contexts to choose from, but based on this unit students will probably suggest:

- school
- work
- being in a shop or café
- being with someone older.

Finally, in order to give examples of when the form is different to its function, there are lots of examples to choose from. Students could choose:

Willy: They're working on a very big deal.

Here, the form is a statement but the function, or Willy's intention, is to ask for his old job back, e.g. 'Can I go to Boston for you?'

T: I want to talk to //you//

Again, Tom's statement has the function of a question, e.g. 'Can we talk about my school?'

Chloë: this is a funded policy the point is (.) the real //point is//

Here Chloë Smith wants to stop talking about the funding of the cut and to focus on its benefits, so her statement has an imperative intent, e.g. 'stop talking about the funding of the fuel tax'.

Mr D: do you think I'm amused

Mr Drew's question has the function of an imperative, e.g. 'stop laughing'.

7 Attitudes to spoken language: 'It ain't what you say, it's the way that you say it'

AO focus

AO2:

- Understand variations in spoken language, explaining why language changes in relation to contexts.
- Evaluate the impact of spoken language choices in their own and others' use.

In this unit your students will:

- discuss regional accents and dialects
- identify a range of attitudes commonly held about accents and dialects
- learn about Standard English
- engage in discussion about the changing nature of spoken language.

Key terms

There are no key terms in this unit.

Articles included in this unit

A summary of favourite accents: a poll's findings illustrating how regional accents are often attributed to personality traits such as friendly, sexy or reassuring.

The Lawyer: a section of an article about discrimination against working-class accents in the law profession.

Daily Mail article: Springs Academy in Sheffield where students have been 'banned' from using slang at school. The article shows both sides of the argument.

Emma Thompson: comments on slang.

See pp99–102 for photocopiable versions of these transcripts for students to work on.

Getting started

Speaking and listening

You could use the mind-map from the Student Book and ask students to add to it, or start from scratch. The aim is to encourage students to see that most people have some views about how English is spoken, even if they think that they don't. The discussion acts as a starting point to discuss attitudes in a more considered way.

Accents

As a starter, use a map of Britain and ask students to match accents with regions. The poll on worst/best accents is also a useful starter, as students can decide whether they agree or disagree with the poll's findings.

Poll: accents

This activity considers how accents are important to people's sense of identity.

Activity 1

a i The completed tables linking accents with well-known people will vary depending on students' experiences. Some suggested answers are below:

Geordie	Ant and Dec
Brummie	Cat Deeley
Scottish	Edith Bowman
Scouse	John Bishop
Irish	Christine Bleakley

ii The adjectives used to describe accents are, again, based on prejudice and are useful to create discussion rather than agreement. Discussion should lead towards the question: 'Does your accent matter?'

This next article expands the debate by suggesting that some accents are associated with personality traits and, therefore, people are judged by their accents.

b i Students should identify that a Scottish accent suggests attributes that would be useful in getting a job where being reassuring is important.

ii Students could give a variety of answers including doctors, nurses, etc.

c Students should be encouraged to acknowledge that everyone has an accent, even if their accent sounds the same as most of the people they know. Get students to question why they do not like their accent (if that is the case) or to discuss what their accent sounds like to other regions.

Unit 7 Attitudes to spoken language: 'It ain't what you say, it's the way that you say it'

The Lawyer

This article asks students to engage with a more controversial topic.

Activity 2

a The identification of what 'ethnic minorities' and 'working class' voices might sound like needs to be carefully managed so that students don't make over-generalised comments.

b However, the discussion about the 'Essex barrow boy' should get students to consider how some stereotypes should be challenged. This feeds into Activity 3.

c People with an accent described as 'soothing' may mean that they are chosen to do a job where they have to deal with the public. An accent 'lacking in prestige' may prevent people from securing high-status jobs such as a pilot or doctor.

Dialect

As a starter, you could ask students to jot down any words they use that are considered dialect words. Most students will find this hard to do without prompting, so you could ask them to think of their own versions of the following, all of which still seem to vary from region to region:

- plimsolls, a game of 'it', the place where you are safe in a game of 'it', a bread roll, etc.

Using pictures of items avoids putting words into students' mouths.

Daily Mail: Springs Academy (1)

The article and the activities that follow provide a discussion point about language and context. The article is about a school environment and should be both accessible and relevant to students.

Activity 1

a Get students to clarify what Springs Academy describes as being slang. Students should find it very easy to think of slang or less formal ways of using language.

b **i and ii** These activities check students' understanding of the article, but then quickly move on to evaluating the point of view. Students should explain that slang has been banned because the school believes that it will harm students' chances of getting a job if they use slang. The staff at the school imply that using slang gives a bad impression.

c **i and ii** These activities may result in a discussion that draws on the earlier article about accents and stereotypes.

Speaking and listening

This exercise is accessible, but students will have to be careful that their use of language is standard and that they avoid any colloquialisms or slang.

Daily Mail: Springs Academy (2)

These next activities are still based on Springs Academy but this article offers an alternative view.

Activity 2

a Students should identify how the banning of slang is not necessarily a useful policy. They should explain that there are several points to Ms Smith's argument, including:

- it is too hard to check up on
- slang and dialect are grey areas and the school will need to identify specific words to ban if the policy is to work
- it is not up to a school to pronounce that dialects are wrong
- it may cause conflict and friction between students and staff
- it isn't necessary; students know when to change their language to suit their audience.

b Discussion of a 'telephone' voice encourages students to explore their own ability to 'code switch' and they will come up with a range of different contexts when they alter their language to suit the audience.

c The written task can be done in class and, as part of a plenary activity, students could read their letters out. This should allow them time to articulate a personal viewpoint about the school's decision.

It's like just bare wrong, innit?

Emma Thompson

This article is a good starter in terms of opening a discussion about different attitudes to slang across the generations. The activities alongside the article will get students to confront and explain their own prejudices.

Activity 1

a **i and ii** Many students may have pet hates such as 'innit' or specific slang words. At this level, most discussion remains anecdotal and can become rather circular, so the following activities are intended to ask students to consider different arguments about slang so that they can discuss the issue in an informed manner.

GCSE Spoken Language Skills
Section A: Spoken language skills

b One way of organising feedback about the Emma Thompson article is to ask students to list arguments for and against. They should then be able to explain whether they agree or disagree with these viewpoints, and suggest areas where their own opinions have changed as a result of reading the arguments.

c Students will draw on earlier discussions to explain whether or not there are some cases in which 'correct' English is seen as important. They will probably identify the fact that many people 'code switch' and are able to recognise when to use slang and when to use correct forms.

For	Against
The danger of young people using language like that is that people assume they're somehow stupid. And that isn't true.	Of course there's a place for modern slang. Language, by nature, is dynamic and it shouldn't always be formal.
There are so many more influences, such as American TV shows and the net, on children that make our jobs as English teachers much more difficult.	Language is always evolving. 'Proper' English approved by the Oxford dictionary – as opposed to slang or colloquialisms – would still eventually evolve because the way we use words always changes.
Language is a melting pot and there are loads of influences on it. But bad influences are contributing to making English teaching difficult.	Yesterday's slang is today's Standard English – some slang words become accepted into formal English and others die out.
Slang gives the impression that younger people don't understand how to use language properly when that's far from the case.	In certain situations, Standard English is not as expressive as slang; it's not as emotional.

Plenary activity

As part of a plenary activity for this topic, students could use whiteboards to say whether they agree or disagree with Emma Thompson's initial viewpoint, citing at least two reasons in support of their view.

Stretch yourself

Get students to work independently in researching meanings as well as people's opinions about a range of less popular slang words. This research could be presented as a graph or chart.

Scheme of work

The language of education: teachers and students

Timeline	Overview	Key learning	References to Teaching Advice	References to relevant pages in the Student Book
Lesson 1: Introduction to non-fluency features	• Speaking and listening: *Just a Minute* activity in Teacher Book. • Discussion and collecting ideas: why do we lack fluency in spoken language? What factors might make us less fluent? • Use the annotated transcript from the Student Book to illustrate how spontaneous speech has specific features and flag up how these are marked. • Use various transcript sample(s) from Student Book Unit 1 on non-fluency to identify and explain non-fluency features.	• Identify features in spoken language. • Develop knowledge of spoken word terminology.	p1 (Just a minute activity); pp2–3 (mind the gap, answers); pp56–7 (Unit 1, transcripts)	pp1–2 (Unit 1, annotated transcript); pp3–6 (Unit 1, Mind the gap, activities)
Lesson 2: Introduction to interaction	• Talking to others: how is your language different when talking to your friends and when talking to adults you don't know so well? Consider: amount you talk, when you talk, words you use, fluency of your speech, quality of your language. • Analyse a blank version of the Kiss FM interview in Student Book Unit 2 to introduce ideas such as phatic communication and back-channelling. This exercise also builds on the semantics, hyperbole and metaphor, to create a friendly and cooperative tone. Focus analysis on language as a reflection of relationship.	• Analyse influence of relationships on language use. • Describe turn-taking strategies. • Infer speakers' intentions based on language choices.	pp63–4 (Kiss FM, transcript)	pp16–17 (Unit 2, annotated transcript)
Lesson 3: Introduction to lexis	• Making predictions based on context: what sort of language would you expect to be used in a consultation between a hairdresser and their client and why? • Use a blank version of the transcript at the start of Student Book Unit 3 to explore formality of lexis. Flag up where predictions were accurate. • Write a script for a specific context, being aware of the use and importance of word choices. • Swap scripts: identify use of specific types of words suited to context.	• Analyse word choices linked to purpose, audience and context. • Use terminology to describe lexical and semantic uses of language.	p72 (hair salon, transcript)	pp32–3 (hair salon, annotated transcript)
Lesson 4: Lexis in school: we're all specialists	• Work through the short activities based on the science lecture transcript in Student Book Unit 3. • What jargon do you know? List the specialist language associated with the school subjects you take. • Work through the activities based on the *Kes* play script in Student Book Unit 3.	• Identify examples of specialist language use. • Analyse and evaluate effects of specific lexical forms.	p13 (science lecture, answers); p13 (*Kes*, answers)	p34 (Unit 3, science lecture, activities); p35 (Unit 3, *Kes*, script, activities)

GCSE Spoken Language Skills
Section B: Schemes of work

Timeline	Overview	Key learning	References to Teaching Advice	References to relevant pages in the Student Book
Lesson 5: Scripting school: what's real and what's not?	• Use a variety of extracts from *Our Day Out*: student talking to another student; teacher to student; teacher to teacher. • How realistic is the language used? • Where it is not very realistic, why might this be? • Alternatively/in addition, use online clips of scripted school-based dramas such as the BBC's *Waterloo Road*.	• Identify differences between scripted and spontaneous forms of spoken language.	p76 (*Our Day Out*, excerpt)	
Lesson 6: Scripting school: larger than life characters	• Study *The Inbetweeners* transcript. • How do these characters come across to the audience? What words would you use to describe their feelings/attitudes/personalities based on this short exchange? • Focus on implied meaning in spoken language: the subtle ways we can convey our thoughts and feelings without being direct. Use the introduction in Student Book Unit 6 and annotations of *The Inbetweeners* transcript to model how to write about implied meanings. • Students explore a range of situations when implied language can have dual meanings and can lead to misunderstandings. Use the section '"That is not what I meant": implied meanings and misunderstandings' in the Student Book for guidance.	• Understand concept of implied meaning. • Infer meaning in spoken language from context.	p93 (*The Inbetweeners*, transcript); pp28–9 (Unit 6, 'That is not what I meant', answers)	p72–3 (*The Inbetweeners*, annotated transcript); pp73–4 (Unit 6, 'That is not what I meant', activities)
Lesson 7: Interactions in school: who's in charge here? (1)	• Create a power chart. What powers does a primary school teacher have in comparison to the children they teach? • Analyse the language used in the primary school transcript at the end of Student Book Unit 1. How does the teacher put pressure on the child to admit his wrongdoing? Annotate the text. • Model how to convert annotations to PEE-style paragraphs. Use some of the model answer from the Teacher Book as an example. • Students can write their own and peer mark.	• Identify features of language linked to power and persuasion. • Write analytically using appropriate terminology.	p6 (teacher – child interaction, model answer)	p15 (teacher–child interaction and counting task)
Lesson 8: Interactions in school: who's in charge here? (2)	• Showing authority in language: being assertive in the right way. Identify problems with given examples of teacher-classroom language and suggest alternatives. • Watch selected clips of Gareth Malone's *Extraordinary School for Boys* (three-part BBC series). Analyse Malone's style of communicating: advantages and disadvantages. Consider tone, gesture, word choices, formality, etc.	• Evaluate effects of a variety of language features.		

Scheme of work The language of education: teachers and students

Timeline	Overview	Key learning	References to Teaching Advice	References to relevant pages in the Student Book
Lesson 9: Interactions in school: who's in charge here? (3)	• Discussion: how might a teacher of GCSE or A Level students use language compared with a primary-school teacher interacting with a Year 5/6 class? • *Jamie's Dream School*: watch selected clips (whole programmes available on 4od, clips on YouTube). Be aware, some clips contain strong language. • Compare strategies used by different teachers and reactions of students, e.g. Alistair Campbell's lesson on advertising v. David Starkey's history lesson.	• Discuss and understand the influence of audience age range on language choices. • Evaluate language used to engage with a teenage audience.		
Lesson 10: Scripted interactions in school: disrupting the usual patterns (1)	• Use the *Oleanna* script excerpts and the range of accompanying activities from Student Book Unit 2 to explore how language can reflect shifts in power and different agendas.	• Identify features of language linked to power and attitude.	p71 (*Oleanna* script, excerpts); p11 (Unit 2, *Oleanna*, answers)	pp29–31 (*Oleanna*, activities)
Lesson 11: Interactions in school: disrupting the usual patterns (2)	• Watch the first episode of *Educating Essex*. What are Mr Drew's tactics for dealing with difficult students? • Use the transcript from Student Book Unit 6 to explore power struggles in the classroom environment.	• Evaluate language used to manage others.	p93 (*Educating Essex*, transcript); p29 (Unit 6, *Educating Essex*, answers);	p29 75–6 (Unit 6, *Educating Essex*, activities)
Lesson 12: Controlled assessment preparation	• Prepare for controlled assessment: analysis of how teachers can use language to communicate effectively with their students. Consider a variety of situations, giving examples of what teachers might say and how they might say it. • Alternatively, use a source such as *Educating Essex* to provide specific scenarios and a range of examples.	• Write analytically about the spoken language of teachers, considering the influence of context on their choices and the impact their choices have on the listener.		

Scheme of work

The language of home and family

Timeline	Overview	Key learning	References to Teaching Advice	References to relevant pages in the Student Book
Lesson 1: Introduction to non-fluency features	• Use the annotated transcript from Student Book Unit 1 to illustrate how spontaneous speech has specific features. • Identify and explain non-fluency features.	• Identify features in spoken language. • Develop knowledge of spoken word terminology.	p1–2	p1–2
Lesson 2: Introduction to lexis	• Use the annotated transcript set in a hairdressers to explore formality of lexis. Write a script for a specific context, being aware of the use and importance of specialist lexis.	• Analysis of registers. • Use terminology to describe lexical and semantic uses of language.	p12	p32
Lesson 3: Introduction to interaction	• Use the annotated example of the Kiss FM interview to introduce ideas such as phatic communication and back-channelling. This exercise also builds on the semantics, hyperbole and metaphor, to create a friendly and cooperative tone.	• Describe turn-taking strategies. • Infer speakers' intentions.	p7	p16–17
Lesson 4: Introduction to implied meanings	• Study The Inbetweeners transcript and identify examples of when language has to be implied. Students discuss a range of situations when implied language can have dual meanings and can lead to misunderstandings. Use the section '"That's not what I meant": implied meanings and misunderstandings' in the Student Book for guidance.	• Discuss language and implied meanings, inferring language from context.	p28	p72–3
Lesson 5: Depictions of home in sitcoms	• Students think of examples of home on television and in sitcoms in particular. Create a list of shows and discuss how stereotypes are maintained or challenged. Watch excerpt from The Simpsons and discuss roles.	• Involvement in discussion. Using evidence to back-up ideas.		p28
Lesson 6: Focus on a sitcom	• Watch an excerpt from another sitcom that features family dynamics: Malcolm in the Middle, My Family or a longer section from The Simpsons. Analyse the way in which characters assume roles of power and confidence within the family.	• Close analysis of language. • Identify aspects of power and dominance and discuss.		
Lesson 7: Lexis and generational differences (1)	• Read the articles from Student Book Unit 7 which start with Emma Thompson's views on slang. Discuss the viewpoints and identify the arguments made by Ian McNeilly and Ted Duckworth.	• Discuss language issue. Identify viewpoint in a written text.	p36	p90

Scheme of work The language of education: teachers and students

Timeline	Overview	Key learning	References to Teaching Advice	References to relevant pages in the Student Book
Lesson 8: Lexis and generational differences (2)	• Using the Student Book activities in Unit 7, identify the way in which slang has changed over generations.	• Discuss language issues, research skills.	p36	p90
Lesson 9: Death of a Salesman	• Use the Student Book activities in Unit 6 to explore family relationships between siblings and parent/child.	• Comment on the writers' views and purposes. • Explore how a text is crafted for an audience.	p31–2	p81–4
Lesson 10: Conflict in families	• List sources of conflict in families. Discuss the depiction of conflict in spoken texts. Watch family arguments in EastEnders and Coronation Street. Homework task to transcribe a family argument.	• Discuss issues. Identify what conflict is.		
Lesson 11: The Family	• Using the transcript from The Family, explore how Tom uses language to present a different sense of self to different parents.	• Close focus on implied meanings and how persuasive language works in speech.	p30	p78–80
Lesson 12: Controlled assessment preparation	• Using The Family transcripts, discuss the question: 'How are family roles and relationships in the TV programme The Family established through language?'	• Use terminology to evaluate spoken language and its impact on others.	p30	p78–80

GCSE Spoken Language Skills
Section B: Schemes of work

Scheme of work

The language of interviews

Timeline	Overview	Key learning	References to Teaching Advice	References to relevant pages in the Student Book
Lesson 1: Introduction to non-fluency features	• Speaking and listening: *Just a Minute* activity in Teacher Book. • Discussion and collecting ideas: why do we lack fluency in spoken language? What factors might make us less fluent? • Use the three short transcripts from the 'Mind the gap' section in Student Book Unit 1. • Either use activities in the Student Book to guide learning or look at all three transcripts side by side, identifying a range of examples of non-fluency. Provide terminology to describe the various features as they emerge.	• Identify features in spoken language. • Develop knowledge of spoken word terminology.	p1 (*Just a Minute*, speaking & listening task); pp56–7 (Unit 1, Mind the Gap, transcripts); pp2–3 (Unit 1, Mind the Gap, answers)	pp3–6 (Unit 1, Mind the Gap, activities)
Lesson 2: Introduction to interaction: getting started in two-way conversations	• Initial mind mapping/discussion: what makes a conversation polite and friendly? • Use the section 'Opening and closing cues' in Student Book Unit 2 as a guide to exploring opening and closing sequences and phatic communication. • Compare tier 1 and tier 2 transcripts from the section 'Maintaining interest' in Student Book Unit 2 to explore the role of back-channelling.	• Identify structural features in spoken interaction. • Develop knowledge of spoken word terminology.	pp7–8 (Unit 2, Opening and closing cues, answers); pp68 (Unit 2, Maintaining interest, transcripts); pp9–10 (Unit 2, Maintaining interest, answers)	pp17–21 (Unit 2, Opening and closing cues, activities); pp25–8 (Unit 2, Maintaining interest, activities)
Lesson 3: Interviews: asking questions and drawing out answers	• Use an un-annotated version of the hobbies interview from the introduction in Student Book Unit 1. Flag up the use of overlapping marks in this transcript. • Annotate the transcript, focusing on the ways in which the interviewer uses language to get her interviewee talking more willingly. • Model PEE paragraphs (use the annotations in the Student Book for ideas). • Students can write their own and peer mark for accurate use of terminology and sufficient explanation of detail.	• Identify examples of language use for purpose. • Write analytical paragraphs using appropriate terminology.	pp55–6 (hobbies interview, transcript)	pp1–2 (hobbies interview, annotated transcript)

Scheme of work
The language of interviews

Timeline	Overview	Key learning	References to Teaching Advice	References to relevant pages in the Student Book
Lesson 4: Interviews: building rapport (1)	• Table of notes and discussion: how is your language different when talking to your friends and when talking to adults you do not know very well? Prompt students to consider: amount you talk, when you talk, words you use, fluency of your speech, quality of your language. • Analyse a blank version of the Tulisa Kiss FM interview from the introduction in Student Book Unit 2. The interviewer has only met Tulisa a couple of times; explore how a feeling of familiarity is created (e.g. through compliments, informal language, back-channelling, pronoun use and mirrored phrasing).	• Analyse influence of relationships on language use. • Describe turn-taking strategies. • Infer speakers' intentions based on language choices.	pp63–4 (Kiss FM, transcript)	pp16–17 (Kiss FM, annotated transcript)
Lesson 5: Interviews: building rapport (2)	• Discussion: celebrity talk shows. Why do celebrities usually go on these shows? How are they usually treated? • Use the section 'Loaded words' in Student Book Unit 3 to explore emotive lexis, connotations, exaggeration and other forms of emphasis. • Use the chat show transcript from Student Book Unit 2. Identify the ways in which Letterman is using language to dramatise the footballer's experiences.	• Develop knowledge of terminology. • Identify lexical features in spoken language used for specific effect.	pp15–16 (Unit 3, Loaded words, answers); p70 (chat show interview, transcript)	pp41–4 (Unit 3, chat show transcripts & activities)
Lesson 6: Interviews: building rapport (3)	• Select three online clips from different talk shows (e.g. Alan Carr; Oprah Winfrey; Michael Parkinson) focusing on the first few minutes of the interviews. • Look for patterns in language and structure that seem common to all three. • Look for differences in style of language used by the three interviewers. • Evaluate the effectiveness of the three interview styles.	• Analyse and evaluate interview structure and style.		
Lesson 7: Interviews: power struggles and gaining control (1)	• Mind mapping/discussion: how can you show authority through language? • Alternatively, use the Speaking and listening task suggested in Teacher Book Unit 1. • Use the committee meeting transcript in Student Book Unit 1 and the accompanying activities to explore ideas of power and control in interactions.	• Develop knowledge of turn-taking and interruption. • Identify features of language associated with power.	p5 (Unit 1, Speaking and listening activity); (Unit 1, committee meeting, answers); p61 (committee meeting, transcript)	pp12–13 (Unit 1, committee meeting, activities)

GCSE Spoken Language Skills
Section B: Schemes of work

Timeline	Overview	Key learning	References to Teaching Advice	References to relevant pages in the Student Book
Lesson 8: Interviews: power struggles and gaining control (2)	• Find an online clip of a celebrity interview where there is a power struggle, e.g. Jonathan Ross-David Walliams-Simon Cowell interview. In this instance, there are three fairly competitive egos interacting. How is their power struggle evident in the interview? Does Jonathan Ross lose his position of power as the host? • Guide students in their note taking or provide them with specific features to tally or watch out for depending on the level of support needed.	• Analyse the ways in which personality and status affect interactions.		
Lesson 9: Interviews: responding to power	• In pairs, script an interaction for a typical job interview. • Annotate to explain how language has been used to suit the purpose, audience, roles of the participants. • Compare the language used in the two interview scenarios in the part-time waiter interview from Student Book Unit 1 and the reception job interview from Student Book Unit 2. • Sum up/share similarities and differences between anticipated language use and the real-life examples.	• Use knowledge of spoken language to predict language features in context. • Synthesise ideas from a range of examples for comparative purposes.	p58 (waiter job interview, transcript); p69 (reception job interview, transcript)	
Lesson 10: Interviews: under pressure (1)	• Use the bank manager meeting transcript from Student Book Unit 3 to explore both the bank manager's techniques for putting Owen under pressure and Owen's strategies for dealing with this pressure. Use the linked activities in the Student Book as a starting point.	• Identify confrontational and evasive conversational strategies.	p75 (bank manager meeting, transcript); pp13–14 (Unit 3, bank manager meeting, answers)	p36 (Unit 3, bank manager meeting, activities)
Lesson 10: Interviews: under pressure (2)	• Use the Channel 4 interview with Chloë Smith from Student Book Unit 6 to introduce political/journalistic interviews. • Analyse Krishnan's interview technique: how many questions are actually questions? What does he tend to do instead? What effect does this have on Chloë Smith? Overall, would you class his style as 'pushy but polite' or 'pushy and rude'?	• Identify grammatical structures used in interviews and explain effects. • Justify interpretations of language use.	p94 (Channel 4 News interview, transcript); p30 (Unit 6, Channel 4 News interview, answers)	pp77–8 (Unit 6, Channel 4 News interview, activities)
Lesson 11: Interviews: under pressure (3)	• Use clips of *Newsnight* interviews to compare Paxman's technique and his interviewees' responses, e.g. Jeremy Paxman and Chloë Smith v. Jeremy Paxman and Boris Johnson. • Explore the reasons for these different responses to Paxman.	• Identify and discuss variations in language use in context. • Evaluate factors that might generate variation.		
Lesson 12: Controlled assessment preparation	• Prepare for controlled assessment: analysis of how interviewers use language to draw out particular responses with their interviewees. Consider a variety of situations, giving examples of what interviewers might say and how they might say it. • Alternatively, use a source such as a news programme, chat show, etc. to provide specific scenarios and a range of examples.	• Write analytically about the spoken language of interviews, considering the influence of context on their choices and the impact their choices have on the listener.		

Scheme of work

Studying the language of reality television

Timeline	Overview	Key learning	References to Teaching Advice	References to relevant pages in Student Book
Lesson 1: Introduction to non-fluency features	• Use the annotated transcript in the Student Book to illustrate how spontaneous speech has specific features. Identify and explain non-fluency features.	• Identify features in spoken language. • Develop knowledge of spoken word terminology.	pp1–2	pp1–2
Lesson 2: Introduction to lexis	• Use the annotated transcript set in a hairdressers to explore the formality of lexis. Write a script for a specific context, being aware of the use and importance of specialist lexis.	• Analyse registers. • Use terminology to describe lexical and semantic uses of language.	p12	p32
Lesson 3: Introduction to interaction	• Use the annotated example of the Kiss FM interview to introduce ideas such as phatic communication and back-channelling. This exercise also builds on the semantics, hyperbole and metaphor, to create a friendly and cooperative tone.	• Students describe turn-taking strategies and infer speakers' intentions.	p7	pp16–17
Lesson 4: Introduction to implied meanings	• Study *The Inbetweeners* transcript and identify examples of when language has to be implied. Students discuss a range of situations when implied language can have dual meanings and can lead to misunderstandings. Use the section '"That's not what I meant": implied meanings and misunderstandings' in the Student Book for guidance.	• Discussion of language and implied meaning, inferring language from context.	p28	pp72–3
Lesson 5: Sport on the radio	• Analysis of the radio phone-in show from Student Book Unit 2. The focus is on how language is used to create interest for the listener and to encourage participation.	• Close reading of language features. • Identify parts of speech and figurative language.	p9	p24
Lesson 6: TV commentary of tour of Britain	• Analysis of the features of television commentary. Imagine what watching sport would be like without the commentary. Explore the roles of the commentators in making sense of the race.	• Identify tense and verbs. • Explore the role of commentary in television.	p25	p66
Lesson 7: Reality TV	• Discussion of reality TV shows. Discuss how viewers are involved in making decisions based on spoken language and speech styles, often in a competitive context (e.g. *Big Brother*).	• Discussion of spoken language and context.		

GCSE Spoken Language Skills
Section B: Schemes of work

Timeline	Overview	Key learning	References to Teaching Advice	References to relevant pages in Student Book
Lesson 8: Prejudice in reality TV	• Discussion of how reality TV can exploit prejudices about accent and language use generally. Use the article about accent in Student Book Unit 7 to explore how identity can be linked to accent and dialect.	• Engage with concepts of accent and dialect. Read opinion piece and synthesise viewpoint.	p34	pp86–7
Lesson 9: Conflict in reality TV	• Watch reality TV show *World's Strictest Parents* and discuss how language use can cause conflict. Explore how structures are used by parents to command control and the difficulties of maintaining these controls.	• Use turn-taking terms to analyse spoken language and control.		
Lesson 10: *Supernanny*	• Watch some episodes of *Supernanny* and explore the way in which parents adapt their speech for children.	• Discussion of language and context.		
Lesson 11: *The Family*	• Using the Student Book activities in Unit 6 as a starting point, explore how Tom in *The Family* uses language to speak to his mum in order to persuade her of his views.	• Identify patterns and tone in conversation.	p30	pp78–9
Lesson 12: Controlled assessment preparation	• Using a range of excerpts from *The Family*, explore how Tom uses language with his mum compared to his dad.	• Close analysis of spoken language for the controlled assessment.	p30	pp78–9

Scheme of work

Analysing scripted language

Timeline	Overview	Key learning	References to Teaching Advice	References to relevant pages in the Student Book
Lesson 1: Introduction to non-fluency features	• Use the annotated transcript from the Student Book to illustrate how spontaneous speech has specific features. Identify and explain non-fluency features.	• Identify features in spoken language. • Develop knowledge of spoken word terminology.	pp1–2	pp1–2
Lesson 2: Introduction to lexis	• Use the annotated transcript set in a hairdressers to explore formality of lexis. Write a script for a specific context, being aware of the use and importance of specialist lexis.	• Analysis of registers. • Use terminology to describe lexical and semantic uses of language.	p12	p32
Lesson 3: Introduction to interaction	• Use the annotated example of the Kiss FM interview to introduce ideas such as phatic communication and back-channelling. This exercise also builds on the semantics, hyperbole and metaphor, to create a friendly and cooperative tone.	• Describe turn-taking strategies. • Infer speakers' intentions.	p7	pp16–17
Lesson 4: Introduction to implied meanings	• Study *The Inbetweeners* transcript and identify examples of when language has to be implied. Students discuss a range of situations when implied language can have dual meanings and can lead to misunderstandings. Use the section '"That's not what I meant": implied meanings and misunderstandings' for guidance.	• Discuss language and implied meaning, inferring language from context.	p28	pp72–3
Lesson 5: Spontaneous v. scripted	• List specific examples of the differences between spontaneous speech and language used for entertainment purposes. Look at the *Friday Night Dinner* script and explore how the writers use spoken language that is close to spontaneous speech but is also crafted for an audience.	• Discuss ideas, identifying implied meanings and awareness of context.	p26	p71
Lesson 6: Lexis	• Look at the *Kes* extract from Student Book Unit 3 and discuss how lexis and jargon are used in the extract. Again, explore how writers draw on aspects of spoken and informal speech to create authenticity.	• Close reading of specific words, introduction of terms like 'jargon'.	p13	p35
Lesson 7: Slang and stereotype	• Look at the *Our Day Out* excerpt and use the Student Book activities to discuss how writers use slang to create authentic characters.	• Analysis of the implications of language choices. • Discuss writers' crafting of characters.	p14	p39

GCSE Spoken Language Skills
Section B: Schemes of work

Timeline	Overview	Key learning	References to Teaching Advice	References to relevant pages in the Student Book
Lesson 8: Attitudes and opinions	• Read the articles about Sheffield's Springs Academy. Identify the different points of view about slang and write a letter to the *Daily Mail* to illustrate your viewpoint.	• Identify viewpoint in a non-fiction text. • Use written language to convey opinion.	p35	pp88–9
Lesson 9: Turn-taking and conflict	• Read the *Oleanna* excerpts and explain what the turn-taking conveys to the audience about the writer's intentions.	• Use spoken word terminology. • Identify subtext and implied meanings.	p11	pp29–31
Lesson 10: Speaking and listening activity based on *Oleanna*	• Role play a teacher and student conversation using some of the features identified in the *Oleanna* excerpts.	• Develop a role, using features from discussion to sustain role.	p11	pp29–31
Lesson 11: *Death of a Salesman*	• Use the Student Book activities to explore how Miller uses spoken language features to create tension and reveal family relationships.	• Comment on the writers' views and purposes. • Explore how a text is crafted for an audience.	pp31–2	pp81–3
Lesson 12: Controlled assessment preparation	• Analysis of how writers use spoken language features to create interesting and realistic characterisations.	• Write analytically about writers' intentions using knowledge of spoken language to inform analysis.		

Scheme of work

The language of different social groups

Timeline	Overview	Key learning	References to Teaching Advice	References to relevant pages in the Student Book
Lesson 1: The basics of spoken language	• Looking at the basics of non-fluency. Use the section 'Mind the gap' in Student Book Unit 1 as an introduction.	• Work with transcripts. • Identify key features and functions of non-fluency.	pp2–3	pp2–9
Lesson 2: Types of talk	• Looking at the different types of talk used in a normal day. Use the introductory activities in Student Book Unit 5 to gain a sense of different forms of spoken language.	• Reflection and note-taking. • Write analytically. • Small group work.	pp22–3; pp24–5	pp58–63; pp63–9
Lesson 3: How talk is organised	• Looking at how talk is organised. Use the introductory activities and the section 'Opening and closing cues' from Student Book Unit 2.	• Work in pairs/small groups. • Identify language use. • Write notes.	pp7–8	pp17–21
Lesson 4: Grammar and structure of talk	• Looking at the structures used in different kinds of speech. Use the introductory activities in Student Book Unit 4.	• Reading and annotating transcripts • Rewriting tasks	pp17–19	pp45–51
Lesson 5: The language of different social groups	• Look back at 'like' and its use among different people. • Use the activities from the section 'Mind the gap' in Student Book Unit 1, which focus on *TOWIE* and different regions and age groups.	• Interpret different meanings for the same features. • Read transcripts for meaning. • Write analytically about spoken language.	pp2–3	pp3–6
Lesson 6: Street talk (1)	• Focus on lexis discussed in the section 'Street talk' in Student Book Unit 3. • Discussion of slang used by different age groups and slang particular to certain regions and areas.	• Discuss in pairs. • Work with word definitions and meanings. • Research skills.	pp14–15	pp37–41
Lesson 7: Street talk (2)	• Use the slang extracts from Student Book Unit 7. • Use links from the SFX Language blog (http://englishlangsfx.blogspot.co.uk/2012/02/playground-prescriptivism.html) to focus on arguments about slang. • Set up a class debate on slang: 'Does it have a place in schools?' • Differing arguments can be written up and used as preparation for controlled assessment on attitudes to slang.	• Group work. • Speaking and listening task.	pp35–6	pp87–90

GCSE Spoken Language Skills
Section B: Schemes of work

Timeline	Overview	Key learning	References to Teaching Advice	References to relevant pages in the Student Book
Lesson 8: Technical talk (1)	• Focus on lexis discussed in the section 'Getting technical' in Student Book Unit 3. • Discussion of technical language and jargon used in specific occupations. • Try using extracts from episodes of *The Big Bang Theory*, *The Great British Bake Off* and *Top Gear* to focus students on the technical language of science, baking and cars.	• Analyse different registers of language. • Focus on appropriate uses of different levels of language.	pp12–14	pp33–6
Lesson 9: Technical talk (2)	• The language of professions. • Use links from http://englishlangsfx.blogspot.co.uk/2010/11/woop-woop-its-sound-of-gavversboy-dempo.html to start a discussion about jargon used by different occupational groups: doctors, teachers, the police and the army. • Split students into small research groups with each group working on the jargon of a different occupational group They present their findings to the class.	• Research and group planning. • Presentations to class.	pp12–14	pp33–6
Lesson 10: Age and language (1)	• Focus on how age influences use of particular features of language. Discussion of quotatives in Student Book Unit 4. • Recording/transcribing own data to use in controlled assessment.	• Write analytically. • Note-taking and preparation. • Respond to feedback and develop own writing skills.	p19	pp49–51
Lesson 11: Age and language (2)	• Preparation for controlled assessment. • Dummy run of controlled assessment question, based on language use of different age groups.	• Write analytically. • Note-taking and preparation. • Respond to feedback and develop own writing skills.		
Lesson 12: Controlled assessment preparation	• Preparation for Controlled Assessment.	• Write analytically.		

Scheme of work

Attitudes to spoken language use

Timeline	Overview	Key learning	References to Teaching Advice	References to relevant pages in the Student Book
Lesson 1: Attitudes to spoken language	• Use the introductory activity in Student Book Unit 7.	• Discuss. • Speaking and listening task.	pp34–5	pp85–7
Lesson 2: Accent (1)	• Use the material in Student Book Unit 7 on accent.	• Reading for meaning. • Comprehension. • Note-taking and analysis of article.	pp34–5	pp85–7
Lesson 3: Accent (2)	• Finding other accents. • Split students into groups to find extracts of different UK regional accents. Ask them to find three or four recordings from a range of areas: Newcastle, Manchester, Leeds, Bristol, London, Essex, Leicester, Birmingham, Gloucestershire, Cornwall, South Wales, Glasgow, Northern Ireland and Liverpool. • Ask students to prepare a five-minute guide to the accent, its features and its most famous users.	• Research. • Note-taking.	pp34–5	pp85–7
Lesson 4: Accent presentations	• Groups present their research into regional accents. • Students are then asked to rate 10 of these accents in order of likeability.	• Speaking and listening task. • Note-taking. • Discuss accents and attitudes to them.	pp34–5	pp85–7
Lesson 5: Dialect	• Use the material in Student Book Unit 7 on dialect.	• Analyse standard and non-standard features. • Write about lexis and register. • Reflect on dialect forms.	p35	pp87–9
Lesson 6: Dialect and accent reduction	• Use the stimulus text from Student Book Unit 7 ('School bans slang!') as a basis for debate on non-standard forms and how they are used.	• Speaking and listening task. • Debate. • Note-taking to prepare for controlled assessment.	pp36–7	p88

GCSE Spoken Language Skills
Section B: Schemes of work

Timeline	Overview	Key learning	References to Teaching Advice	References to relevant pages in the Student Book
Lesson 7: Standard and non-standard	• Writing task: use the letter-writing task in Student Book Unit 7 to focus students on constructing clear arguments about language use, and persuading others of place of different forms of language.	• Write persuasively. • Reflect on audiences and meanings.	pp36–7	p89
Lesson 8: Age and usage	• Use the Emma Thompson article in Student Book Unit 7 and the associated activities.	• Assess others' views. • Respond to different views about language. • Discuss in groups and as a class.	pp36–7	p90
Lesson 9: Slang research	• Carry out paired/small group research into etymologies of slang terms. • Ask students to prepare handouts on individual slang terms. Present these as a class display.	• Research. • Presentations. • Preparing informative handouts. • Note-taking.	pp36–7	p90
Lesson 10: Multimodal gripes	• Use the different multimodal forms in Student Book Unit 4 to look at a range of texts, tweets and other CMC forms. • Use the articles from SFX Language blog (http://englishlangsfx.blogspot.co.uk/2012/02/playground-prescriptivism.html) to start a discussion about attitudes to texting.	• Assess others' views. • Develop ideas and viewpoints about appropriateness of different CMC forms.	pp20–1	pp54–7
Lesson 11: Controlled assessment preparation (1)	• Gather together different arguments about language. • In small groups prepare arguments for and against slang, texting, accents and dialects.	• Speaking and listening presentation. • Note-taking to prepare for controlled assessment.		
Lesson 12: Controlled assessment preparation (2)	• Prepare for the controlled assessment by working on models of analytical sentences, examples of quotations and references to wider ideas from the study of spoken language.	• Write analytically.		

Scheme of work

Multimodal language: tweets, texts and technology

Timeline	Overview	Key learning	References to Teaching Advice	References to relevant pages in the Student Book
Lesson 1: What is multimodal communication?	• Looking at the basics of CMC. • Use the section 'Multimodal texts' in Student Book Unit 4.	• Analyse language. • Discuss new technologies and modes of communication.	pp20–1	pp54–7
Lesson 2: Multimodal forms (1a)	• Texting: looking at the use of spelling, punctuation, abbreviation and ellipsis in Student Book Unit 4. • Analysis of text message styles.	• Write analytically. • Small group work. • Reading and comparing language data.	pp20–1	pp54–7
Lesson 3: Multimodal forms (1b)	• Small group research and data gathering. • Students collect a range of examples of texts and present these to the class.	• Research. • Presentations. • Note-taking.	pp20–1	pp54–7
Lesson 4: Multimodal forms (2a)	• Tweets: looking at the use of spelling, punctuation, abbreviation and ellipsis in Student Book Unit 4. • Analysis of Twitter styles.	• Write analytically. • Small group work. • Reading and comparing language data.	pp20–1	pp54–7
Lesson 5: Multimodal forms (2b)	• Small group research and data gathering. • Students collect a range of examples of tweets and present these to the class.	• Research. • Presentations. • Note-taking.	pp20–1	pp54–7
Lesson 6: Multimodal forms (3a)	• Emails: looking at the use of spelling, punctuation, abbreviation and ellipsis, registers and styles. • Find a range of emails – from formal to informal – and analyse in exactly the same way as texts and tweets.	• Write analytically. • Small group work • Reading and comparing language data.	pp20–1	pp54–7
Lesson 7: Multimodal forms (3b)	• Small group research and data gathering. Students collect a range of examples of tweets and present these to the class.	• Research. • Presentations. • Note-taking.	pp20–1	pp54–7
Lesson 8: Multimodal forms – comparative analysis	• Written work on different forms of multimodal communication. • Written task comparing tweets, texts and emails to written and spoken texts.	• Write analytically. • Reflect on own writing and developing skills.	pp20–1	pp54–7

GCSE Spoken Language Skills
Section B: Schemes of work

Timeline	Overview	Key learning	References to Teaching Advice	References to relevant pages in the Student Book
Lesson 9: Other multimodal forms	• Looking at the language of online gaming, online text commentaries, MSN and Facebook. Use examples from Student Book Units 4 and 5 and own/students' examples.	• Discussion. • Note-taking and analysis.	pp20–1; p25	pp54–7; 67–8
Lesson 10: Arguments about technology	• Discussion of attitudes to texting and young people's spelling and punctuation. Use example articles on SFX Language blog (http://englishlangsfx.blogspot.co.uk/2012/02/playground-prescriptivism.html) to start a discussion on the 'decline' of standards due to texting. • Prepare notes to help with controlled assessment. • Ask students to find other examples of these arguments and prepare a presentation and handouts for next lesson.	• Class discussion. • Note-taking. • Research.		
Lesson 11: Controlled assessment preparation (1)	• Presentation of findings from Lesson 10. • Class to share handouts and make notes to prepare for controlled assessment on attitudes to texting.	• Speaking and listening presentation. • Note-taking to prepare for controlled assessment.		
Lesson 12: Controlled assessment preparation (2)	• Prepare for the controlled assessment by working on models of analytical sentences, examples of quotations and references to wider ideas from the study of spoken language.	• Write analytically.		

Appendices – Spoken language transcripts

1 Non-fluency features: Making it up as you go along

Non-fluency features – an annotated example (pp1–2)

Interviewer: all right (.) erm (.) so what about internet and TV (.) does that take up a lot of your time (1) like spending a lot of time online

James: I'd say it takes about ninety per cent of my life

Interviewer: [laughter] //right//

James: //on Facebook// or the internet

Interviewer: right Facebook (.) so what do you do when you are on (.) what do you do when you are online

James: erm well (1) er a lot of times I am on like forums and things (.) just looking at links and (.) stupid pictures basically

Interviewer: [laughter] //random stuff//

James: //stupid stupid// stuff I can't really explain (.) obviously you can't (.) can't make excuses for something so silly but er (.) yeah just doing that looking at silly sites //basically//

Interviewer: //yeah// YouTube

James: YouTube //a lot of videos and//

Interviewer: //yeah seeing videos//

James: yeah I do er yeah that's about it really (.) just //random sites//

Interview: spontaneous speech (p2)

Interviewer:	//OK// (1) Hayley are you online a lot as well
Hayley:	yes
Interviewer:	(.) what do you do
Hayley:	erm I (.) I have to check my emails about 20 times
Interviewer:	oh yeah oh I am like that [laughter]
Hayley:	an hour erm [laughter] yeah even even when I am at work I try to check my emails erm and also I use it a lot for for research (.) for my course
Interviewer:	oh sure sure
James:	I do that too I'd like to say
Interviewer:	//[laughter]//
Hayley:	//[laughter]//
James:	//I mean I've// got loads it is good for downloading journals and things

At a beauty pageant: Miss South Carolina responds to a question (p3)

Audience member: recent polls have shown that a fifth of Americans can't locate the US on a world map (.) why do you think this is

Miss South Carolina: I personally believe (.) that (.) US Americans are unable to do so (.) because er some er (.) people out there in our nation don't have maps and er I believe that er our ed education like such as in South Africa and er the Iraq everywhere like such as and (.) I believe that they (.) should (.) er our education over here in the US should help the US or or should help South Africa and should help the Iraq and the Asian countries so we will be able to build up our future for our children

The Only Way is Essex: two girls chatting (p4)

L: I love this stage you know like right at the beginning of a relationship and like (.) you get like all excited and like your belly goes round like a washing machine and you get all butterflies

D: I'm so happy for you

L: so we went to like this little Italian in Soho

D: aaw

L: yeah which was really **nice** (.) and then

D: you're blushing

L: what am I

D: yeah you're like [looks up to sky and waves head side to side] ah in the clouds

L: and then we went (.) cinema

D: aaw when you speak about him your eyes are //like (.) all// lit up

L: //do I//

D: yeah they really are you look happy have you kissed him

L: we've had like a little kiss but

D: like a peck

L: like (.) like

D: an adult kiss

L: yeah

D: yeah aaw

Reality talent show: contestants explain their experiences and friendship (p5)

J: I've always had sort of problems with my size since like (.) I can remember (.) and (.) when I was in sort of primary school it was back then really that I had sort of the mick taken out of me and it it kind of damaged my confidence quite a bit (.) when when people would say something to me (1) I'd just (1) it'd just take a little piece out of me in a sense

C: I'm quite protective of Jonathan like (.) if someone (.) if I was there and someone stood there and said something to him (.) I wouldn't sit (.) I couldn't sit there with my mouth shut (.) before you make a judgement of someone I think you really need to get to know them it's not (.) as clichéd as it is it's not judging a book by its cover you've got you've got to read what's inside

J: Charlotte's been a really big help for me in terms of confidence and (.) making me a better performer and I really don't think I'd be going up on stage today if I didn't have Charlotte by my side

A job interview: an applicant thinks on his feet (p7)

Annie: ok (.) right (.) you know the restaurant a bit already then so (.) what made you apply

John: well (1) I was (.) I've always done part-time waiting from when I was young from about 13 or 14 (.) but more local pubs and little places you know (.) but now we've moved into town and it's easier to get to places like this and I'd quite like to work somewhere where it's a bit more formal

Annie: formal in what sense

John: oh (.) well (.) I mean that it's form. well really smart and the food is a bit more special //and//

Annie: //mhmm//

John: the the staff always seem erm I suppose professional compared to some places like they really do a careful job and look after people

Mother and daughter interaction: fitting a hearing aid (pp7–8)

J: it doesn't (.) the aid (.) the aid (.) //doesn't work//

D: //let's have// (1) a look (2) I think it's (2) I think it's (.) twisted (2) hold (.) hold still (1) I need to line it (.) up

J: no good (1) nothing (2) //nothing//

D: //keep still//

J: it's the battery (1) is it the battery

D: no (.) no (.) that's ok (2) it needs to erm fit into your erm ear right (.) it's moulded to your erm to fit your ear

J: no (1) no (1) //nothing //

D: //it's not in// yet (1) Mum (.) Mum hold still (.) should just (1) slot in (1) there (2) how's that Mum how's that

J: what

D: can you hear me

J: yes

D: is it ok (1) comfortable

J: no (.) take it out (.) take it (.) out

D: I give up

Friends disagree: criticising and back-tracking (pp8–9)

A: we need to go (.) are you gonna make a decision

N: I have

A: (1) are you really wearing that

N: what does **that** mean

A: no I didn't mean erm it **is** a nice dress

N: yeah (.) I just look ///horrible// in it is //that it //

A: //no//   //no no// it's nice it's nice I just thought erm (.) isn't it a bit (.) annoying for a party

N: why (.) what do you mean annoying

A: well the skirt bit is quite you know a bit big (.) puffy

N: (1) big and puffy (.) ok (.) //thanks//

A: //no I// just thought well it's (.) it is at their house isn't it

N: yeah so (.) it's a party

A: well you look quite you (.) you look quite I don't know quite dressed up (.) I just thought you might be not be very **comfy** //and//

N: //ok fine// (.) I'll get changed again then shall I

The Jonas Brothers: recounting an unusual event (pp10–11)

K: oh my gosh (.) **coolest** story **ever** about the show last night (1) //you were there//

N: //oh yeah oh yeah//

K: ok I get to tell it //I get to tell it I//

J: //oh cool we should we should//

N: //we're gonna put it up on YouTube// today

K: are we really

N: I think we are

J: we should just bring the video in here and show everybody

K: //ah well//

N: //we won't// worry about that

K: check it out this is the way it's gonna happen (1) so (.) it was //unbelievable//

N: //this is what// happened

K: we were all in the centre ring //we're spinning around//

J: //waah waah awesome//

K: and all of a sudden Nick finishes burning up he's like **bam** I'm done with the song and all of a sudden this dude in the audience gets this pair of sunglasses from //these two girls//

N: //it wasn't out// of anger or //anything//

K: //oh no//

N: he wasn't being mean or anything

K: he was //he was just trying to (.) because the girls said//

J: //he was trying to give Nick a nice pair of yellow// sunglasses (.)

K: so what he did //was//

J: //lime green//

K: [. . .] took these sunglasses and he chucked it as hard as he could (.) and literally (.) they come flying they were like //[rotates hands and makes sound effect]//

J: //amazing//

K: right into Nick's hand like right at Nick's face and he just bam grabs it (.) and then like pulls it and like breaks the glasses and throws them on the ground

N: well I grabbed them so tight in my hands they cracked and then I threw them on the ground

K: it was literally the most like (.) James Bond moment I think you've ever //had//

N: //it was// it was pretty crazy

A committee meeting: conflict in discussion (pp12–13)

Mr Bhatt: next item on the agenda (.) resolution determining committee roles and responsibilities

Ms Martin: (2) ok well I'll make that motion

Mr Bhatt: motion made by Ms. Martin (2) we're waiting for a second (6) still waiting for a second

Mr Wilson: you ought to know you're not going to get one

Ms Martin: it needs discussion //so that//

Ms Hewitt: //no one// wants to discuss this now

Mr Bhatt: I think (.) //it would be better//

Mr Wilson: //you've already// made your speech (.) and frankly (.) we don't need to hear it again (.) you're not going to get a second on this

Ms Martin: //but this//

Ms Hewitt: //so the// motion **fails**

Mr Bhatt: hold on (.) we must follow procedure here

Ms Hewitt: sorry but but the motion fails for lack of a second

Mr Bhatt: hmm

Ms Hewitt: it fails for a //lack of//

Mr Bhatt: //I **understand**// Ms Hewitt

Ms Hewitt: so how long are you going to wait (.) I'm just asking the question how long are you gonna wait

Mr Bhatt: well (2) I'm still waiting for a second (5) //still waiting for a second//

Mr Wilson: //this is ridiculous//

Ms Hewitt: Chairman is there any time limit on (.) how long you have to wait before a motion fails for lack of a second (.) or are we going to sit here till midnight

Mr Bhatt: there's no time limit the the committee has the right to make a motion as it does in all other //instances//

Ms Hewitt: //ok _ ne// (.) is there any procedure er that we can do to end this

Mr Bhatt: well of course if the committee determines that the time needed for making a motion is over someone can make a motion to determine that there has been no second and move on to the next //item//

Ms Hewitt: //ok// I'll make that motion that there has been no second ample time has been given and er it fails for lack of a second

Ms Olson: I'll second

Ms Hewitt: thank you (1) so can we vote please and move on

A family breakfast scenario: multiple conversations (p14)

M: here (4) there (.) here we are (.) slowly (2)

F: Tom (2) //Thomas//

M: //come on// Tom (.) there's a good careful

F: what a mess

M: there we go (.) is it good Tom (.) is (.) does it taste nice Tom (.) that's right all in Tom's tummy (2)

F: what's school what have you got at school today (1) Katie

M: listen to him (.) yummy yummy Tom's tummy

F: are you getting the eight ten (.) sorry school Katie

K: well there's science (4)

F: what are you doing in (.) science

K: leaves and things (2)

F: you getting the eight ten

M: uh huh

F: what have you learnt //about leaves//

M: //there we go//

K: photosynthesis

M: just like that

F: what's photosynthesis then

M: um what's photosynthesis Katie

K: the sun and the leaves (.) something

F: Tom

M: just the one more (.) what does the sun do (.) to leaves

K: erm (.) makes them grow (.) and makes them green (.) chlorophyll or something

M: well let's get you all done

F: right

M: well trees are very important (.) aren't they Tom

2 Interaction and the structure of talk: Following the rules

Kiss FM radio interview with Tulisa (pp16–17)

C: ok so the female boss is in the Kiss building, it's Tulisa

T: hello

C: are you good

T: I'm good how are you?

C: I'm fine thank you (.) so at this moment how are you feeling right now

T: a bit tired

C: laughs

T: I'm always a bit tired at the minute but no I'm all right

C: but tiredness is good it means you're still working (.) still doing it=

T: =exactly (.) I'm getting a few days off so I'm looking forward to that now

C: what you gonna do on your days off

T: literally just go to sleep and chill out with mates and just //relax//

C: //and// just sleep

T: sleep a lot (.) sleep a lot and eat food and //watch DVDs//

C: //you're a girl// after my own heart like the sound of that now last time I interviewed you it was about a year ago (.) X Factor was just about to air (.) you were hinting about this solo career that you have started now and now here you are so has the past year kind of surpassed your expectations

T: defnitely what I can't me (.) I can't complain what a year it's just been amazing obviously with everything from the X Factor um to now releasing my solo stuff it's just a whirlwind like I dunno pinch me someone pinch me I dunno //what's going on//

C: //I can't quite reach over//

T: there you go=

C: =there you go it's real=

C: on that note Tulisa thank you very much for hanging with us

T: thank you for having me

C: May 7th all about it (.) Young (.) go get it

T: wicked

Opening and closing cues (p18)

B: can I help

A: two cokes and a blueberry muffin please

B: anything else

A: no thanks

B: £5.80 then

A: there you go

B: thanks and 20 pence change

A: thanks bye

B: have a good day

The Only Way is Essex: a conversation showing the use of phatic communication subtext (p19)

S: hello

M: how you doin'

S: good thanks you (3) mm make-up looks good

M: how you getting on

S: not bad

M: you look nice

S: thanks

M: good outfit

A telephone conversation: two lovers saying goodnight (p21)

M: night darling (.) sounds like you're dragging an enormous piece of string behind you with hundreds of tin pots and cans attached to it (.) I think it will be your telephone (.) night night before the battery goes (blows kiss) night

W: love you

M: don't want to say goodbye

W: neither do I (.) but we must get some sleep (.) bye

M: bye darling

W: love you (.) hopefully talk to you in the morning

M: please

W: bye (.) I do love you

M: night

W: love you forever

M: g'bye (.) bye my darling

W: bye (.) press the button

M: going to press the button

W: all right darling

M: night

W: night

M: love you

W: (yawns) love you

M: adore you (.) night

W: (blows a kiss)

M: night

W: g'night my darling

M: (disconnects the call)

Transactional or interactional? Conversations in a greengrocer's/at home/in the canteen (p22)

Text 1
In a greengrocer's

A: isn't it bitter (.) really cold

B: really cold (.) yeah so (.) haven't seen a spring like it for years

A: no (.) years

Text 2
At home

A: are you watching this (1)

B: shut the door

A: oh you're nice

B: shut it

A: I want to watch *Friends*

Text 3
In the canteen

A: do you know where the French workroom is (.)

B: no (.) don't do French um it's on the third floor I think

A: oh (.) I'll try up there then

An interactional conversation: two girls discussing their websites (p23)

A: anyway (.) as my website was great (.) I had like seven different pages Leah had only five

L: //I wasn't here for one of them//

A: //so// (.) you could have done two pages=

L: =I did, I did more than that (.) I had like seven or eight (.) //more than you//

A: //Ooh you// embarrassed me in front of the tape

S: our one's called //stars site//

A: //anyway// mine had loads of information Leah's just was all just like Olly Murs' middle //name//

L: //I had//

S: //ooh// what's Olly Murs' middle name (.) I don't //know//

L: //and other// stuff

A: oh yeah I have like lots of events and stuff (.) you can have your birthday party there right next to the llamas um you can have your wedding and it says something like this er do I hear wedding bells ringing=

L: =you decide=

A: =the lions roaring=

L: =(laughing) you decide

talkSPORT radio phone-in show: how presenters use language to involve their listeners (p24)

JC: hello good evening and welcome to the Sports Bar here on Talk Sport with me Jason Cundy and my wingman for the next 3 hours Mr Sam Delaney coming between now and 1 am we'll be discussing Andy Carroll (.) I know we broke the news last night but it looks like a likely move away from Anfield (.) Liverpool fans do you want to see him go and West Ham Chairman David Sullivan has said that he wants to take him on (.) would you have him at your club call 08717 22 33 44

SD: we will also be joined by new Reading signing Nicky Shorey and taking your calls on tonight's match between England and Australia (.) all that plus tomorrow's back pages.

Back-channelling: a lack of feedback (p25)

A: how's your mum and dad

B: fine

A: is your mum still working (.) at the post office

B: no

A: oh (.) when did she leave

B: dunno

Back-channelling: examples (p26)

C: I had a tat (.) of his name

H: (laughs)

C: and two weeks later we split up

H: two weeks

C: yeah had it and almost broke up straight away

H: did you (.) god two weeks

C: yeah an (.) and then it was like (.) I can't believe it

H: really

Back-channelling and its purpose in maintaining interest in conversations (p27)

Director: the company's been going for about **24 years** (.) did you look us up on the website

Interviewee: I did **yeah yeah** (.) yes I did actually {clears throat} it's a global company so (.) erm when your assistant rang me I said I was interested in gettin' into a global company again (.) cause it's quite big //and//

Director: //yeah//

Interviewee: and you do get obviously //take a// (.) great amount of **calls** and everything

Director: //yep yep//

Interviewee: and it's //it's a busy **role** and//

Director: //yeah absolutely very//

Interviewee: and I you know I used to run two switchboards in the one (.) for Barclays at Gadbrook **Park** and erm (.) the Peterborough one so one was erm (.) you know for wills and that and the other is (.) //an investment so//

Director: //OK mm hmm//

Interviewee: I took anything up to (.) 300 //calls a day//

Director: //right OK//

Interviewee: as well as multi tasking=

Director: =yeah, yeah, oh absolutely

Sportsman on a chat show (p28)

Jake (J): that looks like a pretty nasty injury you have there (.) it's your leg I'm guessing (.) right

Daniel (D): yes

J: so how did you injure yourself

D: um playing for my local team (.) Dagenham Old Boys (.) I went to knock it round the guy and just felt this searing pain and collapsed and the back of my leg was like (.) on fire (.) really really burning and I realised I'd done my er hammy y'know

J: actually completely tore your hamstring muscle (.) torn (.) goodness (.) what a nightmare and er at what point did you know it was serious=

D: straight away (.) straight away er soon as I tried to get back up and play on (.) I felt the rip and er looked down and er I could feel the burning in my thigh spreading all down my leg

J: wow

D: I know (.) yeah (.) proper nasty

J: I was gonna ask you about that that's what people always say (.) and it truly was the experience=

D: yeah (.) yeah

J and perhaps one of the most painful injuries a footballer can endure

***Oleanna*: extracts from the play (pp29–30; pp30–1)**

1.

    John: There are problems, as there usually are, about the final agreements for the new house.

    Carol: You're buying a new house.

    John: That's right.

    Carol: Because of your promotion.

    John: Well, I suppose that's right.

    Carol: Why did you stay here with me?

    John: Stay here.

    Carol: Yes. When you should have gone.

    John: Because I like you.

    Carol: You like me.

    John: Yes.

    Carol: Why?

    John: Why? Well? Perhaps we're similar (pause) Yes (pause)

    Carol: You said 'everyone has problems.

2.

John: No one thinks you're stupid.

Carol: No? What am I . . .?

John: I . . .

Carol: . . . what am I, then?

John: I think you're angry. Many people are. I have a telephone call that I have to make. And an appointment, which is rather pressing; though I sympathise with your concerns, and though I wish I had the time, this was not a previously scheduled meeting and I . . .

Carol: . . . you think I'm nothing. . .

John: . . . have an appointment with a realtor, and with my wife and. . .

Carol: You think that I'm stupid.

John: No. I certainly don't.

Carol: You said it.

John: No I did not.

Carol: You did.

John: When?

Carol: . . . you . . .

John: No. I never did, or never would say that to a student, and. . .

Carol: You said, 'What can that mean?' (pause) 'What can that mean?'. . .

3 Lexis: The words we use

At the hairdressers: hair stylist consulting with a new client (pp32–3)

H: right then what we doing with this haircut

C: right well basically most of the hair like you know coming off it's getting a bit

H: so you're taking (.) right then so how much length are we talking about

C: erm probably to start off with because you can kind of see where I've dyed and highlighted it before kind of up to there

H: so we're talking about a sort of bobby-type length

C: erm yeah kind of a bob but not so much of a bob //in itself//

H: //no//

C: so it's got more //build in it//

H: //no I know but there// are all sorts of variation of bob there's a one-length bob there's a graduated bob there's a layered bob there's a textured bob yeah (1) so what I think we should do then

C: mhmm

H: is put in a nice one length

C: yeah

H: put in a simple few layers

C: mhmm

H: blow-dry it get it perfect and straight

C: mhmm

H: and then texture it (.) and what you'll end up with (.) is a sort of nice dicey

C: yeah

H: choppy textured little number

C: mhmm

H: it's not gonna be one length and boring

C: fabulous yeah

H: but at the same time it's not gonna be layered to death

A science lecture: an expert on a specialist subject (p34)

thank you **all** for (.) coming today [. . .] the aim of these lectures is to [. . .] just cover a **few** of the things that you're gonna be (.) learning about and working on in your GCSE (.) Science just a few of the topics that **we** thought were interesting and you would perhaps want a little bit more **depth** and a little bit more (.) **detail** about erm topics like the formation of the moon er (.) topics like the the earth's magnetic field and what it does for us and how it creates the the northern lights and also (.) er going all the way back to the start of the universe the big bang (.) so what is the evidence for the big bang what (.) **was** it when did it happen (.) but most crucially (.) how do we know

I know that (.) some of you will have (.) learnt about **isotopes** (.) of different **elements** which (.) if you get an element like carbon (.) for example which has **six** protons (.) and **six** neutrons in it (.) that's called carbon-12 because it's got 12 protons and neutrons all put together (.) you can also have a thing called carbon-14 (.) which has **six** protons and **eight** neutrons (.) that's called a different **isotope** same for oxygen and in **fact** (.) it turns out that the **ratio** of these different forms of oxygen in rocks is **very** (.) sensitive it can be very sensitively measured and at different places in the solar system er when planets formed closer to the sun or further away from the sun you find different ratios of these things

Kes: delivering a presentation to the class (p35)

Billy goes out to the front of the class hesitatingly.

Mr Farthing: Right, how did you set about training it?

Billy: I started training Kes when I'd had him about a fortnight. He was as fat as a pig though at first. You can't do much with them until you've got their weight down. Gradually you cut their food down, until you go in one time and they're keen. I could tell with Kes because he jumped straight on my glove as I held it towards him. So while he was feeding I got hold of his jesses.

Mr Farthing: His what?

Billy: Jesses. He wears them on his legs all the time so you can get hold of them as he sits on your glove.

Mr Farthing: And how do you spell that?

Billy: J-E-S-S-E-S.

Mr Farthing: Right, tell us more.

Billy: Then when he's on your glove you get the swivel – like a swivel on a dog lead, then you thread your leash – that's a leather thong – through your swivel, do you see?

Mr Farthing: Yes, I see. Carry on.

Billy: So you wrap your leash round your fingers so Kes is now fastened to your hand. When you've reached this stage and he's feeding from your hand regular and not bating too much . . .

Mr Farthing: Bating . . . what's that?

Billy: Trying to fly off, in a panic like. So now you can try feeding him outside and getting him used to things.

Business interview: jargon under pressure (p36)

Mike: how many (.) mothers have you (.) spoken to to verify that they would **sign up** for (.) this advice service

Owen: direct (.) erm (.) correspondence on this (.) is time-consuming is labour-intensive //and//

Mike: //so// my question is (.) how many mothers of young children have you spoken to (.) about their **willingness** to actually **pay for** a new mother's service

Owen: the proposal has been informed by my partner (.) in the local area the numbers in this demographic are **strong** and the projected uptake of this service will be very high (.) on //a national scale//

Mike: //how many//

Owen: the demand for e-subscription will be even better

Mike: so I just need numbers here

Owen: (1) I haven't con_rmed the exact properties of the service to the target consumer

Mike: so you haven't spoken to any mothers

Owen: **not** for this particular service

Mike: what you're doing is you're asking for investment of _ fty thousand pounds but what you're saying is I **haven't** done the market research **required**

Owen: yes the design process has been the focus and I haven't asked the question (.) will you subscribe to e-Mums but (.) I think it's obvious at this stage that the design is the the key unique selling point

Radio DJ webcast: London DJs using modern slang (p38)

Lennie: alright so listen right something else that **we** like to do on this show is letting people know what is **hot** and what **ain't** ok **swag** we're talking about **swag**

Monique: now obviously you can see Len's in the denim swag

Lennie: and Monique she is **rockin** the red today (.) that's swagalicious right there (.)

Monique: [laughing] ok but there are people we feel need to **update** their swag

Lennie: that's right (.) check out the swag **doctor** and **fix** that illness right so first up (2) Plan B man (.) **really** how many grey suits you got man (.) come on man you look like you been locked out in the rain man (.) **fix up** man put on a hoodie

Monique: you might think we're being a bit harsh but we're gonna go the other way and big up the people who **have** got swag ok

Lennie: oh there's bare people who've got swag (.) right take a look at this

Monique: yes Tinie **Tempah** (.) different **kind** of swag

Lennie: (.) that guy (.) **that's** how you wear a suit man (.) I am feelin that (.) that's how you wear suits Plan B now fix up man

Our Day Out: troublesome students on the bus (p39)

As the coach goes along the city streets the kids are talking and laughing and pointing. On the back seat, Reilly secretly takes out a packet of cigarettes. The little kid sees them.

Digga: Reilly, light up.

Reilly: Where's Briggsy?

Digga: He's at the front, I'll keep dixie. Come on we're all right, light up.

Little Kid: Agh 'ey. You've got ciggies. I'm gonna tell miss.

Reilly: Shut up you an' open that friggin' window.

Little Kid: No . . . I'm gonna tell miss.

Digga: Go'n tell her. She won't do nott'n anyway.

Little Kid: I'll tell sir.

Reilly: You do an' I'll gob y'.

Digga: Come on . . . open that window, you.

Little Kid: Why?

Reilly: Why d' y' think? So we get a bit of fresh air.

Little Kid: Well there's no fresh air round here. You just wanna smoke. An' smokin' stunts y' growth.

Reilly: I'll stunt your friggin' growth if y' don't get it open.

The Wild One: slang from another time (pp40–1)

Kathie: What do you do (1) I mean do you just ride around or do you go on some sort of a picnic or something?

Johnny: A picnic? man you are too square I, I, I'm' a have to straighten you out (1) now listen you don't go any one special place that's cornball style (.) you just go (1) a bunch get together after all week and it builds up (.) you just (.) the idea is to just have a ball (.) now if you're going to stay cool you've got to wail (.) you've got to put something down you've got to make some jive don't you know what I'm talking about?

Kathie: Yeah yeah, I know what you mean.

Music award ceremony: enthusiastic responses (p42)

Music matters to me because it was the one thing that gave me like a a passion a dream a hunger something to really live for you know I think at the end of the day (.) everybody can sort of wake up and get on with their ordinary life but discovering music and falling in love with it made me realise that (.) I had a purpose I had something that I wanted to do and I had something that I had to work my butt off to achieve you know and that's why music matters to me.

Hugh Grant at the Press Standards Enquiry: expressing concern (p43)

I **just** think that there has been (.) a **section** of our press that has become – **allowed** to become toxic over the last 20 or 30 years (.) er its main tactic being bullying and intimidation and blackmail (.) and I think that that needs a lot of **courage** to stand up to and I feel that it's time (.) you know this country has had historically a good record standing up to bullies and I think it's time that this country found the courage to stand up to this bully now.

Football discussion: emphasising ideas (p43)

Jeff: of course the other headline that came out of Chelsea this week was that Ashley Cole (1) brought an air rifle to training and shot a student [sighs] what was he thinking of

Alan: I couldn't tell you Jeff (.) it's the **stupidest** thing I've heard (1) in twenty years of football [. . .]

Charlie: I've heard some (.) absolutely ridiculous stuff (.) but I've never heard of anything as (.) way out as whacky as this

Matt: it's bizarre (.) it's bizarre really unbelievable

4 Grammar and structure: Stories, texts and tweets

College gym instructor: introducing new students to gym equipment (pp45–6)

Instructor: all right guys (.) welcome to the erm (.) college fitness suite (2) before we start the induction (1) we'll be running through some basics about how to sign in at the desk (.) then it will basically be us (.) taking a look at all the equipment (1) pointing out the safety implications of err each piece of equipment and making sure that you can use it all correctly (.) so that when you come to work out for the first time (.) you know what you are doing and you're not gonna cause injury to yourself or others (.)

What I'll get you to do after we've finished is (.) to look at the rules and regulations (.) the type of things we'll expect from you (.) and err one of those err things will be about making sure you bring your ID card with you each time (1) another thing will be about telling us about any injuries or health problems you've got

So, I hope that makes sense (.) is that clear?

Students: <respond by nodding>

Instructor: The first thing I need to stress is that you must use the equipment in the way it's intended (1) you can injure yourself quite badly (.) and damage the equipment if you don't do it properly (1) so you should always do the following (.) on this running machine check the settings first (.) adjust to your stride if necessary (.) like this and then find the right pace

Once you've found the right speed, you can adjust the speed up or down like this (1) but don't go too high too quickly or you'll end up **whoah** (.) flat on your face like that (.) so take it gently yeah (.) and you can set the timer here for either how many kilometres you want to run (.) so like 5k 10k whatever (.) or for how long you want to run (.) ten minutes twenty minutes OK

So, that's pretty much it I hope that's been of use to you (1) any questions please ask me (.) OK guys thanks very much

Customer and sales assistant: conversation in a shop (p47)

C: two of the number 8 scratch cards please and a book of stamps

SA: first or second class

C: first please

SA: 6 or 12

C: err (.) 6 please

SA: anything else

C: no that's great thanks

Story dialogue extract: a girl on holiday (pp47–8)

Jane didn't have much of her holiday money left and wondered if she'd have enough for an ice cream. The ice cream man served the children in front of her and then turned to her.

'What would you like then, my dear?'

'How much are the large cones, please,' she asked.

'They're one pound fifty,' he replied.

That was too much. She only had about one pound twenty left.

'Oh, how much are the small cones then?'

'They're one pound thirty.'

Jane counted out her coins, but it wasn't enough.

'How much have you got there?' asked the man.

'I've got one pound twenty five,' Jane replied sadly.

'That'll do. Just give us that,' said the man and he served her an ice cream.

'Thank you,' said Jane.

Mother and daughter: discussing a stolen phone (p50)

A: I bet she was in a right state

B: it wasn't a lot of fun (.) she was really upset so I said to her come on it's only a phone (.) we can phone up the company and block it and then get you another one on the insurance

A: ah right

B: and she was all right after that (.) I think she was worried it'd be a big problem with the bill or whatever

Zack's bike: a teenager's account (p50)

Zack: no it was like (.) it was the end of school yeah so that school's finished yeah and everyone was going home and I was getting my bike from the bike rack and I was going out and I was riding my bike and he stopped my bike (1) I was like 'yeah' and he goes 'get off the bike' I was like 'why am I getting off the bike I'm going home like I've gotta go home' yeah he was like 'no get off the bike walk the bike outside of school' I was like 'what's the point' yeah cos like it's quite far like to get out the school from the entrance like in the school yeah and he goes 'ah no get off the bike' yeah so like he kind of shoved me off the bike so I dropped it but I didn't fall over like but I kind of stumbled yeah and he put his (.) he tried to take my bike up to his office like he was gonna keep my bike there (.) I was like 'no'

College principal: greeting new students (p51)

P: Hello and welcome to all of you (2) this morning I will be telling you a little bit about what you can expect in the year to come (.) some of the expectations we have of you (.) what you can expect from us (1) I will be introducing you to some of the faces you will be seeing around college during your first few days with us (.) and telling you about some of the things you will need to do over this first induction week (2) but first (.) let me just say how pleased I am that you have chosen Fulchester College to continue your studies and what a wise choice you have made

Radio interview: between a presenter and a video games expert (p52)

P: so your research tells us that there is no direct link between video games and violent behaviour (.) is that about it basically

V: well it's a very complicated picture (.) in fact some research carried out last year seemed to suggest that in a few cases (.) where young people had been playing what might be classed as violent games for at least six to eight hours a day (.) quite extreme cases it has to be said (.) there was an increase in aggressive behaviour (.) however our latest research suggests that it's a murkier picture

Protester's story: eyewitness account (p53)

Basically err (.) I was at Tower Hill tube with Paul (.) err waiting for Gary and Rashid to get there (.) there was like hundreds of people (.) all with placards and banners (.) people were meeting up with their mates (1) I could hear police horses coming closer and then this guy near me shouted they're charging they're charging and it was like **woah** (.) looked round and there was four or five mounted police bombing towards us (.) we just dived out of the way into this newsagents' doorway and they just like swept by (1) don't think I've ever come that close to getting trampled before

Tweets and texts: computer-mediated-communication (pp54–5)

Tambourine_Dream @Tim_Tolby
Wonder why how many of the released QPR player end up at elland rd? #lufc #MOT

Collapse   ←Reply   🗑 Delete   ★ Favorite

8:47 AM – 23 Aug 12 via wed · Details

Jon Cooper @coopzinnit   15
RT @lufcbarmyarmy: Soooo want to believe this!!!! #LUFC www.guardian.co.uk/football/takeover

Details

WesleyHeadley @westheledge   27m
I cant take this no more !!!!
On… off… done… collapsed?
Arghhhh!! Sort it out KB!
#Pen4Ken #lufc #BatesOut

Details

What u doin goin out with him???
Only joking :-O

When is game on? Need to know so can sort lift out

Festival web forum: music fans discussing their favourite performers (p57)

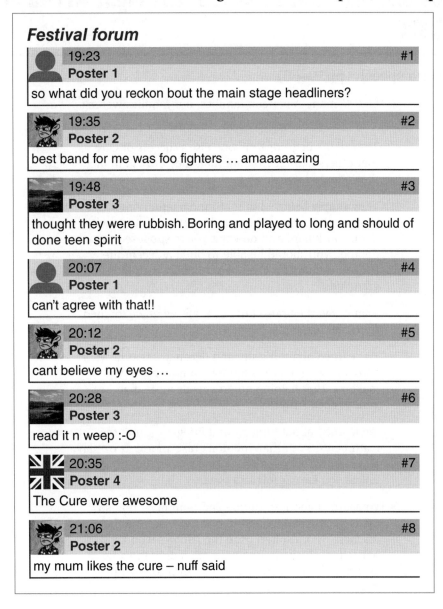

5 Planned and unplanned speech: The right words at the right time

Michelle Obama speech (pp59–60)

Like so many American families, our families weren't asking for much.

They didn't begrudge anyone else's success or care that others had much more than they did . . . in fact, they admired it.

They simply believed in that fundamental American promise that, even if you don't start out with much, if you work hard and do what you're supposed to do, then you should be able to build a decent life for yourself and an even better life for your kids and grandkids.

That's how they raised us . . . that's what we learned from their example.

We learned about dignity and decency – that how hard you work matters more than how much you make . . . that helping others means more than just getting ahead yourself.

We learned about honesty and integrity – that the truth matters . . . that you don't take shortcuts or play by your own set of rules . . . and success doesn't count unless you earn it fair and square.

We learned about gratitude and humility – that so many people had a hand in our success, from the teachers who inspired us to the janitors who kept our school clean . . . and we were taught to value everyone's contribution and treat everyone with respect.

Those are the values Barack and I – and so many of you – are trying to pass on to our own children.

That's who we are.

And standing before you four years ago, I knew that I didn't want any of that to change if Barack became president. Well, today, after so many struggles and triumphs and moments that have tested my husband in ways I never could have imagined, I have seen firsthand that being president doesn't change who you are – it reveals who you are.

You see, I've gotten to see up close and personal what being president really looks like.

And I've seen how the issues that come across a president's desk are always the hard ones – the problems where no amount of data or numbers will get you to the right answer . . . the judgment calls where the stakes are so high, and there is no margin for error.

And as president, you can get all kinds of advice from all kinds of people.

But at the end of the day, when it comes time to make that decision, as president, all you have to guide you are your values, and your vision, and the life experiences that make you who you are.

Bill Clinton script: given to journalists before he delivered his speech (p61)

I understand the challenge we face. I know many Americans are still angry and frustrated with the economy. Though employment is growing, banks are beginning to lend and even housing prices are picking up a bit, too many people don't feel it.

I experienced the same thing in 1994 and early 1995. Our policies were working and the economy was growing but most people didn't feel it yet. By 1996, the economy was roaring, halfway through the longest peacetime expansion in American history.

President Obama started with a much weaker economy than I did. No president – not me or any of my predecessors could have repaired all the damage in just four years. But conditions are improving and if you'll renew the president's contract you will feel it.

I believe that with all my heart.

President Obama's approach embodies the values, the ideas, and the direction America must take to build a 21st century version of the American Dream in a nation of shared opportunities, shared prosperity and shared responsibilities.

Bill Clinton actual speech: delivered in September 2012 (p62)

Now, look. Here's the challenge he faces and the challenge all of you who support him face. I get it. I know it. I've been there. A lot of Americans are still angry and frustrated about this economy. If you look at the numbers, you know employment is growing, banks are beginning to lend again. And in a lot of places, housing prices are even beginning to pick up.

But too many people do not feel it yet.

I had the same thing happen in 1994 and early '95. We could see that the policies were working, that the economy was growing. But most people didn't feel it yet. Thankfully, by 1996 the economy was roaring, everybody felt it, and we were halfway through the longest peacetime expansion in the history of the United States. But – (cheers, applause) – wait, wait. The difference this time is purely in the circumstances. President Obama started with a much weaker economy than I did. Listen to me, now. No president – no president, not me, not any of my predecessors, no one could have fully repaired all the damage that he found in just four years. (Cheers, applause.)

Now – but – (cheers, applause) – he has – he has laid the foundation for a new, modern, successful economy of shared prosperity. And if you will renew the president's contract, you will feel it. You will feel it. (Cheers, applause.)

Folks, whether the American people believe what I just said or not may be the whole election. I just want you to know that I believe it. With all my heart, I believe it. (Cheers, applause.)

Now, why do I believe it?

I'm fixing to tell you why. I believe it because President Obama's approach embodies the values, the ideas and the direction America has to take to build the 21st-century version of the American Dream: a nation of shared opportunities, shared responsibilities, shared prosperity, a shared sense of community.

Xbox Live video game: boys playing the same game, on the same team but in different countries (pp64–5)

L: over there (1) yeah (.) wait (.) **wait**

F: where are they

L: can't see them yet (.) //just//

F: //there look he's coming over (.) he's crossing the bridge=

L: =get him (.) **Get** him quick (.)

F: I need more ammo

L: you've just got to hit him

F: got to get to cover

L: wait (.) cover me (.) he's in the barn (.) you come to me (.) yeah

F: right (.) can't see him (.) where are you

L: by the wall (.) next (.) next to the oil drums (.) you get here and we'll (1) stop (.) wait (.) he's there in the (.) the window

F: who got him

L: what

F: someone got him

L: not me

F: uh-oh

Tour of Britain cycle race: live commentary (p66)

C1: stage 5 of the Tour of Britain will take the riders from Trentham Gardens through to Hanley in Stoke-on-Trent (.) a distance of 147 kilometres (.) and one of the toughest stages (.) they've always proved to be (.) real characters in the history of this race (1) Bradley Wiggins (.)
well just rolling away at the front there with Mark Cavendish (.) in the IG Markets gold jersey (1) ahead of them (.) well (.) a tough test (.) will Cavendish be able to keep the lead

C2: an extremely difficult stage we've got here in Stoke (.) Bradley Wiggins there (.) riding alongside his team leader Mark Cavendish in that IG gold jersey

C1: the flags are out (.) in support in support of Mark Cavendish there's Christian Howes leader in the King of the mountains and riding alongside him Pete Williams (.) leader in the Yodel Sprint competition (3) well here's a shot of the tail of the peloton (.) already the speed is **very** high as you can see **oh there's a crash** (.) now who's gone **ooh** several riders have hit the deck (.) and that's one of the members of the Liquigas team (.) that's Borgini=

C2: =yeah Borgini from Liquigas down (.) and Brett Lancaster there (.) also on the floor (.) facing backwards actually (1) several riders (.) gone down (1) Borgini looks in all sorts of trouble (1)

C1: and also Brett Lancaster the Australian (.) well look at that the tyre absolutely destroyed (.) this is the rider from Orica Greenedge (.) Brett Lancaster (.) and it looks as though he's in serious trouble (.) and Borgini=

C2: =yeah (.) both these riders in no hurry to get back up (1)

C1: well look at this here (.) Cavendish getting some attention to his shoe

C2: yeah obviously a buckle broken there and the mechanic just putting some insulating tape on there to keep his foot in that shoe (.) nice and securely (1)

C1: meanwhile the boss of the peloton Bradley Wiggins says thank you very much boys (.) Cav's back and they start racing

Note: peloton is the main group of riders.

Football: text commentary (p67)

 13 mins GOAL
Bayern Munich 0–1 Real Madrid

In the first game of the group stage, you don't want to give a goal away like this! Angel di Maria curls over a wickedly inswinging corner from the right and Pepe gets the flick-on. Neuer comes out to punch, misses and Benzema is left with a simple tap-in. First blood to the Spanish champions.

18 mins

What a start from Real, they are really playing a clever attacking game. An excellent first-time pass by Alonso almost puts Ronaldo clear down the left, but for the last ditch interception by Philip Lahm.

SOMEONE LIVE *Radio's Alvin Hunsen*

Xabi Alonso and Mesut Ozil seem to have free rein of the midfield and Real look dangerous on the flanks. It feels like it will only be a matter of time before Ronaldo will show his class. It's just great that they've come to give it a good go!

25 mins CHANCE

Against the run of play di Maria dawdles on the ball and Schweinsteiger dispossesses him and Bayern are counterattacking. Martinez moves the ball forward quickly into the box, but Mario Gomez's snapshot lack the precision to beat Casillas, who makes a good sharp save.

SOMEONE LIVE *Radio's Matt Twiddle*

At the moment it looks like Bayern are slowly coming back into the game – Schweinsteiger's influence is growing.

 30 mins RED CARD & PENALTY TO REAL

Ronaldo once again receives the ball in space, on the right this time and he's away and into the box he beats Badstuber for pace and knocks the ball past Neuer who clips the Portuguese's cleverly trailing foot. That's a penalty and referee Olsen reaches for his top pocket. Bayern are really up against it now! An hour with ten men and probably 2-0 down.

Classroom talk: teacher introducing guests to the class (pp68–9)

A: can I introduce some people here (.) who've given up their time and their considerable expertise (.) they work for Saatchi's which is one of the biggest advertising agencies in the world OK (.) they have already (.) been working on your ideas (1) [shows poster to class]

F: [reading from poster of Wayne Rooney] earns 10 times more than a school teacher

B: I like //that//

D: //yeah//

A: Do you like this one= [showing poster of David Beckham]

C: =I love David Beckham

A: yeah

C: what's that say

A: [reading from poster] no I got the snakeskin interior with teak //design//

C: //no that's mean// I like David Beckham

F: [laughter]

A: ok (.) Henry

D: yeah

A: do you remember the other day when you made a speech

D: yeah

A: right what did you make a speech about

D: cannabis

A: cannabis (.) and what did you say about cannabis

D: how it should be legalized=

A: =and what was one of the points that //Danielle// made can you remember

E: //tax// tax

A: correct (.) what do you think of that then [holds up poster]

F: [reading from poster] let's make cash from hash [laughter]

A: any idea you take you can turn into an advert right (.) Now listen (.) Nana-Kwame and Michael (.) you told me (.) you were gonna work (.) on a campaign about knife crime and youth //services// right

G: //yes//

A: this chap over here (.) //right//

G: //the good looking fella//

A: this is Chris right (1) Chris (.) is a designer and he's gonna start to design stuff as we discuss it (.) so Nana-Kwame you start to tell us about your (.) idea you and Michael right (1) what is your point you start telling us your point (.) about knife crime and youth services (.) and this guy will do you an advert

Remote control family talk: a transcript (p69)

A: any idea where the remote for the TV is

B: is that your cup on the floor

C: err (.) yeah

B: why is it lying there

C: I was going to take it back in a minute

D: you always leave your stuff lying around

C: shut up

B: can you help Daddy find the remote please

C: the what

Pigeon English: an extract from the novel (p70)

Miquita was ironing Lydia's hair. Mamma go sound her when she finds out.

Me: I bet it goes on fire.

Lydia: How! No, it won't.

Me: I bet it does.

Lydia: Don't disturb!

Me: I can watch if I want. Lydia can't stop me watching. I'm the man of the house.

Lydia: Just don't burn me, OK?

Miquita: Don't worry, man. I've done it enough times.

Chanelle: Twice.

Miquita: So? I'm well skilful, innit. My auntie taught me, she learnt it in the pen.

Friday Night Dinner: a transcript from the TV show (pp70–1)

M: hi boys

J: what you doing in the garage

M: we're having a clear out

A: don't you mean 'what's Jim doing in our loo'

M: Martin you do know the boys are here (.) say hello

D: what d (.) oh hello bambinos

J: no top tonight

M: he's boiling=

D: =I'm boiling

A: and Jim's using our toilet because=

M: =oh his is broken=

J: =broken

M: he broke it [points to box] no there

A: he broke his own toilet (.) how did he do that

M: how do I know anyway (.) he asked if he could use ours (.) what could I say

A: no

J: use a bucket

D: [points to a pile of magazines] them as well

M: **yes** (.) all of them and you're doing the sofa bed

D: your mother wants me to chuck away all my copies of New Scientist magazine (.) can you believe it

A: yes

M: thank you Adam

D: what do you mean 'yes'

M: you don't even **read** them why do you keep all this crap

D: it's not **crap** (.) I wish you'd stop calling it crap (.) they're collectables

A: are they

D: boys look (.) this one (.) is from 1969 and (.) there's a (.) poster of Isaac Newton (.) now he was a gen//ius//

M: //sorry// I'm not discussing Isaac Newton again (1) tomorrow morning you are taking them all to the dump (.) **impossible**

D: Newton

A: crap

J: crap

6 Implied meanings: Why don't you say what you mean?

The Inbetweeners: an annotated TV comedy script (pp72–3)

Will: Mr Gilbert (.) you seem like an intelligent man

Mr Gilbert: Ah (.) I seem intelligent. How lovely of you to say

Will: No no I just meant

Mr Gilbert: Well I've long been insecure about my capacity for learning so it's nice to have it ratified by you (.) a child

Will: What I meant was (.) do you think that these badges which single us out as new kids are a good idea

Mr Gilbert: Yes (.) and if you have any more views on it I suggest you join the school debating society (.) obviously you'll have to start one first

Spoken Language Skills: phone call (p73)

(Phone call)

Adult: hi. Is mummy there?

Child: yes (puts phone down)

(At a party)

Child: can I have some more Coke?

Mum: don't you think you've had enough?

Child: no

Educating Essex: a reality TV script (p76)

Mr D: I do not wish to experience your unpleasantness so do not make me experience it

C: (laughing) all right

Mr D: am I amused

C: (pointing at a friend) he's laughing at me

Mr D: am I amused

C: don't know are you

Mr D: am I amused

C: don't know are you

Mr D: do you think I'm amused

C: don't know (.) maybe

Mr D: OK we're doing this until you give the correct answer

C: (laughs)

Mr D: will I be amused

C: I don't know cos I'm not you

Mr D: do you think I'll be amused (.) have a guess Charlotte (.) do you think I'll be amused

C: one day maybe I don't know

Mr D: do you think I will be amused

C: oh my God

Mr D: do you think I'll be amused

C: (laughing) I can't stop laughing

Channel 4 News: the presenter and politician Chloë Smith discuss the Government's U-turn on fuel tax (p77)

Krishnan: well earlier I spoke to the Economic Secretary to the Treasury Chloë Smith and I asked her why the Government is spending money that it doesn't have

Chloë: well this is money that will be accounted for of course this is money that is er going to come from departmental underspend and we'll be coming back with more details of that at the Autumn statement

Krishnan: so at the moment it is an unfunded tax cut

Chloë: no this is money that we are gaining from er department underspends as I //said//

Krishnan: //where//

Chloë: we– we as I say from departmental underspend from departments which have underspent and we have a number of those and we'll be able to come back at Autumn statement to give full details //of those//

Krishnan: //so you// don't know at the moment

Chloë: the work is of course progressing to ensure that er it is possible to give you er a full range at the Autumn statement

Krishnan: is it possible that there isn't a half a billion pounds worth

Chloë: we we we are confident we have the er funds available er to make this policy work and the point //is//

Krishnan: //confident// but not certain

Chloë: this is a funded policy the point is (.) the real //point is//

Krishnan: //but// it is not funded because you can't tell me how it is funded

Chloë: the //the//

Krishnan: //you're// thinking it will be

Chloë: I'll be able to give you detail at the Autumn statement

***The Family*: a reality TV programme showing a mother and her son discussing school (pp78–9)**

T: mum can I talk to you about the school thing

M: no (.) you have to talk to dad

T: I want to talk to //you//

M: //no// because I get into trouble

T: I want to talk to you first (.) we'll say that we haven't talked //but//

M: //no// because it always comes out and I get into trouble (2)

T: no (.) well (4)

M: could I be right in thinking you just don't like any school you've been to

T: no but I don't like school

M: oh //well//

T: //they// push you too //hard//

M: //well// because you're a bright boy

T: but they push you too hard

M: but they only expect what they know you can achieve

T: no they don't

M: yeah they do it's just you need to put in a bit of effort

T: I do put in effort

M: when do you put in effort (.) I've never seen you doing any homework

T: that's cos I don't have em

M: that's cos you don't do it

T: I don't wanna be at that school mum I hate it

M: what what

T: I hate it they shout at you for a small thing cos our school is so strict an' all this pressure to do well

M: it's good

Death of a Salesman: three excerpts (p81; p82; p83)

1.

Biff: Why does Dad mock me all the time?

Happy: He's not mocking you, he-

Biff: Everything I say there's a twist of mockery on his face. I can't get near him.

Happy: He just wants you to make good, that's all. I wanted to talk to you about Dad for a long time, Biff. Something's – happening to him. He – talks to himself.

Biff: I noticed that this morning. But he always mumbled.

Happy: But not so noticeable. It got so embarrassing I sent him to Florida. And you know something? Most of the time he's talking to you.

Biff: What's he say about me?

Happy: I can't make it out.

Biff: What's he say about me?

Happy: I think the fact that you're not settled, that you're still kind of up in the air . . .

Biff: There's one or two other things depressing him, Happy.

Happy: What do you mean?

Biff: Never mind. Just don't lay it all to me.

Happy: But I think if you got started – I mean – is there any future for you out there?

2.

Biff: Your hair . . . (He touches her hair) Your hair got so grey.

Linda: Oh, it's been grey since you were in high school. I just stopped dyeing it, that's all.

Biff: Dye it again will ya? I don't want my old pal looking old. (He smiles)

Linda: You're such a boy! You think you can go away for a year and . . . You've got to get it into your head now that one day you'll knock on this door and there'll be strange people here –

Biff: What are you talking about? You're not even sixty, Mom.

Linda: But what about your father?

Biff: (lamely) Well, I meant him too.

Happy: He admires Pop.

Linda: Biff, dear, if you don't have any feeling for him, then you can't have any for me.

Biff: Sure I can Mom.

3.

Howard: Willy, look . . .

Willy: I'll go to Boston.

Howard: Willy, you can't go to Boston for us.

Willy: Why can't I go?

Howard: I don't want you to represent us. I've been meaning to tell you for a long time now.

Willy: Howard, are you _ ring me?

Howard: I think you need a good long rest, Willy.

Willy: Howard –

Howard: And when you feel better, come back and we'll see if we can work something out.

Willy: But I gotta earn money, Howard. I'm in no position to –

Howard: Where are your sons? Why don't your sons give you a hand?

Willy: They're working on a very big deal.

Howard: This is no time for false pride, Willy. You go to your sons and you tell them that you're tired. You've got two great boys, haven't you?

Willy: Oh, no question, no question, but in the meantime . . .

Howard: Then that's that, heh?

Willy: Allright, I'll go to Boston tomorrow.

Howard: No, no.

Willy: I can't throw myself on my sons. I'm not a cripple!

Howard: Look, kid, I'm busy this morning.

Willy: Howard, you've got to let me go to Boston!

Howard: (*hard, keeping himself under control*) I've a got a line of people to see this morning. Sit down, take five minutes, and pull yourself together, and then go home, will ya? I need the office Willy.

7 Attitudes to spoken language: 'It ain't what you say, it's the way that you say it'.

A summary of favourite accents: a poll's findings illustrating how regional accents are often attributed to personality traits such as friendly, sexy or reassuring.

What your accent says about you (pp86–7)

Various pieces of research have suggested that the way we speak has a huge influence on the way we are perceived.

Geordie

Earlier this year, the Geordie accent was voted the sexiest in Britain. Researchers believe celebrities from Newcastle such as Cheryl Cole have helped raised the profile of the accent, making it seem more friendly and attractive.

Scottish

Scots were found to have the most reassuring accents in Britain, in a recent survey. The Royal National Lifeboat Institution made the discovery in a poll asking which accent people found most soothing in emergencies, although the research did not delve into the numerous regional varieties of the Scottish tongue.

Scouse

Liverpudlians fared little better in the BBC's research. The accent was said to be viewed by respondents as 'lacking in prestige' and the second most 'unpleasant' to the ear.

Irish

Last year the Irish accent on men was voted the world's sexiest in a poll of 5,000 women. The popularity of stars such as Colin Farrell were said to be the cause of the accent's popularity.

The Lawyer: a section of an article about discrimination against working class accents in the law profession (p87)

Top firms reject candidates with 'working class accents'
21 December 2010/By Luke McLeod-Roberts

The UK's top law firms are rejecting well-qualified candidates because their accents are too 'working class', according to a new study.

Research carried out by the Cass Business School shows that while elite firms have made strides on increasing recruitment of ethnic minorities into their ranks, working class applicants miss out because they do not fit with the brand.

A partner at one of five case study firms, all of which are in the UK top 20, told Cass Business School: 'There was one guy who came to interviews who was a real Essex barrow boy, and he had a very good CV, he was a clever chap, but we just felt that there's no way we could employ him. I just thought, putting him in front of a client – you just couldn't do it.'

An article from the *Daily Mail* on the use of slang in the classroom (p88)

School bans slang! Pupils ordered to use the Queen's English in the classroom 'to help children get jobs'

By Leon Watson

Parents can breathe a sigh of relief – but the local MP isn't impressed.

A school has ordered youngsters to leave slang at the gates and learn to speak the Queen's English.

Sheffield's Springs Academy hopes to give its pupils a better chance of getting a job, so slang or 'text talk' has been banned while they are on the premises.

The United Learning Trust which runs the school, which has 1,100 students aged from 11 to 18 and is in a working-class area of the city, believes slang creates the wrong impression during interviews.

Kathy August, deputy chief executive of the trust, said: 'We want to make sure that our youngsters are not just leaving school with the necessary A to Cs in GCSEs but that they also have a whole range of employability skills.

'We know through the close relationships we have with business partners and commercial partners that when they are doing interviews with youngsters, not only are they looking at the qualifications, they are also looking at how they conduct themselves.

'What we want to make sure of is that they are confident in using standard English. Slang doesn't really give the right impression of the person.

'Youngsters going to interviews for their first job need to make a good impression so that employers have confidence in them.'

Ms Smith, a former GCSE English teacher at a South Yorkshire secondary, said: 'The school is wrong to ban slang. How will the school police this?

'Who will say what the difference is between slang and dialect? It could completely undermine the confidence of the children at the school.

'If someone tells them how to speak they could dig in their heels and do it all the more. I really think they have set themselves a task that is impossible to achieve.'

Ms Smith said: 'Who is going to adjudicate? Who is going to say slang, dialect or accent? And which one is right and which one is wrong?

'Most people know when to put on their telephone voice because that is what we are talking about. When people go on the phone or talk to anyone in authority they put on a different voice.'

An interview with Emma Thompson, who outlines her support for Standard English at all times (p90)

That Emma Thompson's, like, well annoyed, innit

The Oxford-educated actress has hit out at slang used by the young, claiming it makes them sound stupid when they're not. The 51-year-old, known for her roles in Shakespeare film adaptations, said the use of sloppy language made her feel 'insane'.

'I went to give a talk at my old school and the girls were all doing their "likes" and "innits?" and "it ain'ts", which drives me insane,' she told the *Radio Times*.

'I told them "Just don't do it. Because it makes you sound stupid and you're not stupid." There is the necessity to have two languages – one that you use with your mates and the other that you need in any official capacity.'

Glossary

Adjective: a word used to describe a person, place or thing.

Ad-lib: to make something up on the spot or to say something unprepared.

Back-channelling: the supportive words or sounds that are used to indicate that we are listening and interested in a conversation.

Cohesion: the way that a text or piece of speech holds together through features such as repeated words and structures.

Colloquial: describes language that is chatty and informal but which everyone can understand.

Command: an utterance where one speaker tells another to carry out an action.

Compressed grammar: text that is reduced to some of its most important parts and leaves out bits that can be worked out from the context.

Computer-mediated communication (CMC): a means of communicating that uses some kind of electronic device such as a mobile phone, PC or laptop. It is neither written nor spoken but usually typed on a keypad.

Confirmation checks: words and phrases used to check if the listener is following.

Conjunctions: words used to link together other words, phrases or clauses (e.g. 'and', 'but', 'if').

Connotations: the ideas or feelings associated with a particular word.

Context: the situation in which spoken language is used. It includes factors such as who is interacting, what their relationship is, their purpose, where they are, who is listening, what else is going on around them, and so on.

Context dependent: relying on the immediate environment to make complete sense.

Cue: language that acts as a prompt.

Denotation: the literal, dictionary meaning of a word. This is often different to the connotations the word may have.

Direct: to be explicit in putting forward your thoughts.

Directive: a sentence or utterance acting as a kind of command or order.

Discourse markers: words or expressions that draw listeners' attention to what is coming next.

Dynamic verbs: verbs that describe physical actions.

Ellipsis: missing out words, phrases or larger clause elements.

Emoticon: a symbol used in CMC to express emotion or attitude.

Emotive: describes a word or phrase that provokes a strong emotional response in the audience.

Explicit meaning: the meaning is very clear and there is no room for interpretation. The opposite of implied meaning.

False start: where you start, stop, and then start again in what you say. This often happens at the beginning of an utterance but it can also happen halfway through.

Filler: a word or phrase that does not appear to add much meaning but which might allow the speaker a bit of extra time to think about what they really want to say.

Formal: describes language that is polite, official or complex.

Hyperbole: an exaggerated statement.

Imperative: a sentence that acts as a command.

Informal: describes language that is casual, friendly or unofficial.

Interactional: when the social relationships are more important than the message.

Interrogative: a sentence that acts as a question.

Intonation: the way in which pitch goes up and down in speech.

Jargon: special words or phrases including subject-specific words that are used by a particular profession or group.

Latching on (=): describes conversations where there is no gap between the participant's utterances. A bracket with a dot in the middle (.) is a short pause.

Lexis: a technical term for words or vocabulary.

Metaphor: a word or expression that suggests a comparison with something else but which is not meant literally.

Modal verb: a type of verb that works with a main verb to add a degree of certainty, obligation or doubt.

Oratory: public speaking; skill in public speaking.

Overlapping: talking at the same time as someone else. This can be marked in a number of ways. In this book we have indicated this by placing // at the beginning and end of the overlap.

Phatic communication: a type of warming up; you are getting yourself ready for the demands of the person that you are talking to and the context of the talk.

Primary purpose: the main aim of what you are trying to communicate.

Quotative: an expression used to describe the way in which someone said something.

Register: the style of language used in a particular context; language can have a formal, informal or mixed register.

Repair: changing the wording of what you were originally going to say.

Rhetoric: the art of using language persuasively and effectively.

Scheme: a generally or expected agreed structure to a familiar type of interaction.

Secondary purpose: other aims you might have.

Signposting device: a word or phrase used to help listeners follow the structure of what is being said.

Slang: very informal words and phrases that are used and understood by only certain groups of people.

Spontaneous speech: speech that is not planned or rehearsed.

Standard English: this is the variety of English that is agreed to be grammatically correct and uses vocabulary that is understood by most English speakers, regardless of region.

Statements (declaratives): utterances or clauses that state a point (rather than asking a question or giving a command).

Subject-specific: any words that are closely connected to a specialist subject.

Subtext: similar to an implied meaning and describes the concept that what we say is not necessarily what we mean.

Tone: refers to the emotions behind a speaker's utterance. Tone is created by the sound of your voice, by the pitch, pace and speed that you talk at, and even by the words you choose.

Transactional: when language has a message as its main focus.

Transcript: words written down exactly as they have been spoken.

Turn-taking: the normal structure of conversations in which one speaker's turn (what they have to say) is followed by another's.

Utterance: when someone speaks, we usually refer to each unit of speech as an utterance. This term can be used for very tiny or very long amounts of speech that are said all in one go.

Vague language: expressions typical in speech which are often used to finish utterances or to make the speaker sound less certain.

Voiced pause: a pause in which the speaker makes a sound, for example 'erm'.

Acknowledgements

The author and the publisher would also like to thank the following for permission to reproduce material:

Text permissions pages 57 and 64, extracts from *The Only Way is Essex*, produced by Lime Pictures; p63, Radio interview with *Tulisa Young*, reproduced with permission of KissFM UK; p67, Radio phone-in, talkSPORT; p71, extracts from *Oleanna* by David Mamet; p74, Excerpt from KES adapted by Lawrence Till from Barry Hines' *A Kestrel for a Knave* copyright © 2000 Barry Hines and Lawrence Till. Reprinted by arrangement with the publisher: www.nickhernbooks.co.uk; p76, *Our Day Out* by Willy Russell, sourced from *Studio Scripts – Our Day Out and Other Plays* first published by Nelson Thornes in 1991, last reprint 2010; p76, Screenplay The Wild One by John Paxton and Ben Maddow, first released 1953; p50, text reproduced courtesy of QMU; p80 Kerswill, P., Cheshire, J., Fox, S. and Torgersen, E. (2007). Linguistic Innovators: The English of Adolescents in London: Full Research Report ESRC End of Award Report, RES-000-23-0680. Swindon: ESRC pp84–5, Michelle Obama to the Democratic Party Convention in September 2012; pp85–6, transcript of Bill Clinton's Speech to the Democratic National Convention; p91, *Pigeon English* by Stephan Kelman, published by Bloomsbury, 2011; p92 Extract from *Friday Night Dinner*, Big Talk Productions Ltd; p93, extract from *The Inbetweeners* by Damon Beesley and Iain Morris, Bwark Productions; p94, *Educating Essex*, Channel 4, Twofour Productions; p95, Channel 4 News interview; p96, extract from *The Family*, Series 1, Channel 4; pp97–8, Excerpts from *Death of Salesman* by Arthur Miller. Copyright © 1949, Arthur Miller, used by permission of The Wylie Agency (UK) Limited; p100, extract from *The Lawyer*, 21 December 2010; p101, © *Daily Mail*, 'Schools ban slang! Pupils ordered to use the Queen's English in the classroom "to help children get jobs"' by Leon Watson, 15 February 2012; p102, 'That Emma Thompson's like, well annoyed, innit' reproduced courtesy of *Mirrorpix*.

Every effort had been made to trace the copyright holders but if any have been inadvertently overlooked the publisher will be pleased to make the necessary arrangements at the first opportunity.